SCOTTISH LITERATURE'S
DEBT TO ITALY

Scottish Literature's Debt to Italy

R.D.S.JACK

ITALIAN INSTITUTE, EDINBURGH

EDINBURGH UNIVERSITY PRESS

© Italian Institute, Edinburgh, 1986
Edinburgh University Press
22 George Square, Edinburgh
Set in Linotronic Ehrhardt
by Speedspools, Edinburgh, and
printed in Great Britain by
Clark Constable Ltd, Edinburgh
British Library Cataloguing
in Publication Data
Jack, R.D.S.
Scottish literature's debt to Italy
1. Scottish literature—Italian influence
2. English literature—
Scottish authors—Italian influences
I. Title
820.9'9411   PR8522.I3/
ISBN 0 85224 526 2

Breve Nota
di Introduzione

Gentili lettori,
l'Istituto di Cultura di Edimburgo ha ritenuto di essenziale importanza esplorare, attraverso una serie di iniziative editoriali, i rapporti, le influenze, i prestiti culturali e linguistici, sviluppatisi nel corso dei secoli tra l'Italia e la Scozia.

Questo Paese, anche se ha perduto la sua indipendenza politica, non ha però mai cessato di sviluppare quei caratteri originali che da sempre e per motivi etnici, e per motivi linguistici, hanno caratterizzato una sua precisa identità culturale, artistica, linguistica, nei confronti della confinante Inghilterra.

Il presente saggio esplora, come resulta evidente dallo stesso titolo, i rapporti fra la letteratura scozzese e quella italiana dal cinquecento ad oggi: mi è grato in questa occasione esprimere i miei sentiti ringraziamenti all'autore del saggio Dott. R. D. S. Jack dell'Università di Edimburgo e al direttore della Edinburgh University Press, Archie Turnbull, che con la loro erudizione e con il loro entusiasmo hanno reso possibile questa iniziativa.

L'Istituto di Cultura di Edimburgo si impegna a provvedere in un prossimo futuro alla pubblicazione di saggi a cura dei migliori specialisti locali nelle materie, volti ad approfondire i rapporti tra Scozia e Italia da un punto di vista storico, artistico, culturale, economico e scientifico fino a giungere ad una 'summa' che dia una visione globale delle relazioni fra i due Paesi.

Franco Vicenzotti
Direttore dell'Istituto
di Cultura di Edimburgo

Contents

I

The Field

The aim of this book is a simple one – to provide an account of the major Italian influences on Scottish Literature from the sixteenth-century Renaissance to its modern equivalent. I have been able to present only the briefest study of earlier literature partly on grounds of space but also because, undeniably, major Scottish interest in Italian began only about 1585 when James VI created his Castalian band of court poets in Edinburgh and encouraged them to profit from the great European master-pieces. This is not to deny the presence of possible earlier echoes. Towards the end of the fifteenth century Robert Henryson's *Orpheus and Eurydice* proves suspiciously close to Poliziano's *Orfeo* but there are dating problems and the parallels, while many, are not perhaps specific enough to constitute a definite interrelationship. Yet, even if one cannot accept the *Orfeo* as a direct source for Henryson, it is clear that both authors are working within the same neoplatonic traditions. They interpret the tales in the same way, employ imagery with the same signifi-cances and see the power of music and the harmony of the soul as centrepoints of the myth.

About the same time there appeared a linked group of tales entitled *The Thre Prestis of Peblis*, usually now attributed to John Reid of Stobo. Reid appears to have spent some time in Italy and wrote letters to Rome. As a result it is scarcely surprising to find that one of the tales told in the collection (that of Maister Archebald) is in essence that of Giletta di Nerbona related by Boccaccio as the ninth story of the third day in *Il Decamerone*. The possibility of other influences remains. The link tale of the disguised jester reminds me of the third tale in Franco Sacchet-ti's *Il Trecentonovelle*, where Parcittadino, a grain-sifter from Lin-ari, becomes Court Jester and in this capacity visits King Edward of England. If this work is not in fact a source it is at least a very close analogue.

Gavin Douglas in *The Palice of Honour*, composed about 1500, shows in his Court Rhetoricall, that he is impressed by the contribution of Italian writers and humanists, most notably Pet-rarch, Boccaccio and Bruni. His awareness of the feud between Poggio and Valla is also conveyed in the following lines:

And Poggius stude with mony girne and grone
On Laurence Valla spittand and cryand fy!

In many ways both the ideas behind and the overall form of *The Palice* are reminiscent of Petrarch's *Trionfi*. In particular the opening and closing scenes are close but as the poem is based on a progression, which by then was conventional, and as there are other possible sources, it is perhaps safest to see the Italian line as one whose importance should be noted but not overstressed.

In the mid-sixteenth century, the work which most obviously encourages us to think of Italian connections is *The Dreme* by Sir David Lindsay of the Mount, more famous as the author of *Ane Satyre of the Thrie Estaitis*. As a courtier, he had at an early age visited Italy, passing the following poetic compliment to Italian women:

> To se I think ane plesand sicht,
> Of Italie the Ladyis bricht,
> In thair clething maist triumphand
> Above all uther christin land.

The Dreme was written in the 1520s, that period when the poet is believed to have visited Italy, and most critics think that he borrowed the general idea for his work from Dante's *La Divina Commedia*. Certainly both poets endure a long winter's night ('la notte ch' i' passai con tanta pietà'). Surrounded by barrenness, a symbol of their spiritual state, they try to escape through climbing and meet respective guides in Virgil (Dante) and Dame Remembrance (Lindsay). As they both pass through Hell, Purgatory and Heaven the reader is likely to be more impressed by dissimilarities than similarities and to contrast Dante's consummate craftsmanship with the faltering stanzas of the youthful Scottish poet. But the overall debt is clear and at times verbal parallels remind us how seriously Lindsay took the guidance offered by *La Commedia*.

In the remaining periods, still acutely aware of limitations on length, I have chosen to study in some detail those figures who I consider to be of major importance, either because of their obvious genius or because they made a vital historical contribution to the development of Scottish/Italian letters. Lord Byron, for example, gains entry on the first count, William Fowler on the second. This approach enables me to give something other than a superficial account and prevents the essay from becoming merely a checklist.

Three other decisions on method should be noted. As there are so many examples of Italian writers influencing Scots, it seemed unfortunately necessary to focus on those alone, ignoring the undoubted examples of influence working in the other direction. We know of the debt owed by Manzoni and Grossi to Scott;

of the tremendous Italian popularity of Thomson's *Seasons*, of *Ossian* and, today, of the mutual influence of Scots on Sicilian poetry; Sicilian on Scots. These are most important features but they must be the topic of another book.

Secondly, I have not always confined myself to specifically literary influences. My study of the novel in particular convinced me that Scottish writers who had lived for some time in Italy used their knowledge of that country to produce Italian settings, which might not have quite the force of Egdon Heath in Hardy's *Return of the Native* but certainly play a dramatic part in works as disparate as *South Wind* and *The Takeover.* Douglas, Mackenzie, Spark, Linklater, and Massie are novelists of quality and their contribution seems to me just as important within the modern period as the closer poetic translations of Montale by Morgan or Belli by Garioch.

It is part of the perceived function of the modern section of the book to explore these different types of Italian influence, relating them to the very different historical backgrounds perceived by Scottish poets and novelists, the one group looking over their shoulder at an almost embarrassing array of earlier Italian riches; the others at a halting, late and uncertain tradition. Different situations produce different – highly intriguing – solutions and my attempt to grapple with this quite complex situation is one reason for the final decision on method – devoting almost half of the book to the twentieth century. There are other reasons. It is my belief that now the two literatures are working together as thoroughly and fruitfully as at no other time except James VI's Renaissance in the late 1500s and early 1600s. Also, a book whose audience are not necessarily interested only in academic discussions may well find the challenge of 'Where now?' more exciting than that of 'Once thus'. I cannot tell, but having earlier written on all the periods except the modern one, I have certainly found my researches in this neglected area extremely stimulating.

James VI and the First Renaissance

The fact that James VI, when taking over government of Scotland in 1585, decided that Scottish letters had fallen away badly from the halcyon days of Henryson and Dunbar is now widely known, as is his creation of a group of court poets (the Castalian Band) under his patronage. The ideals of this band in some ways proved encouraging to those interested in Italian letters. Among the works which James possessed and used in framing his critical trumpet blast for the new movement ('The Reulis and Cautelis') was *La Poetica* of Trissino. Also the King's determination to produce verse distinct from that written in England guaranteed a European dimension to his experiment. Indeed, he went so far as to suggest to his major poets that they each translate or imitate one great foreign masterpiece. So far so good. But the franco-phile reign of Mary, the laureate poet Montgomerie's admiration for Ronsard and James's own preferences for Du Bartas and Desportes guaranteed that, for the most part, writers within the group would turn to France for inspiration.

¶ Fortunately there proved to be two major exceptions to this rule. The first was John Stewart of Baldynneis, a man whose exact origins were a matter of some concern at court. Although officially the second son of John Stewart, 4th Lord Innermeith and Elizabeth Betoun, he was believed by many courtiers to be James VI's bastard. His subsequent career is marked by wrongful imprisonment, bitter legal battles with the crown and a growing sense that although he was in the court he was not of it. Yet at an earlier and happier time he had proudly proclaimed himself James VI's poetic disciple and presented to the monarch one of the finest existing sixteenth-century Scottish manuscripts, con-taining all his works to date and especially his *Roland Furious*.

I have in another context argued in some detail the relationship between this 'Abbregement . . . translait out of Ariost' and the *Orlando Furioso*. Essentially we may say that Stewart used not only Ariosto but material from Desportes' *Roland Furieux* and *Angélique*. He also used, in areas not covered by Desportes, the French prose translation of Jean Martin, first published in 1543. But close analysis also proves that he was by no means confined to French intermediaries, having read Ariosto in the original. This technique of reading the major source as well as all available translations and adaptations mirrors the thoroughly professional practice of other Castalians, notably William Fowler and James himself.

But what did he think of it? What impression did Ariosto's highly imaginative work make on this particular member of James's band? Readers of Stewart would agree that in most of his works he controls his highly ingenious, even virtuosic rhetoric by placing it within a clear, analytic overall structure. That being the case, it will come as no surprise that he found the seemingly endless plots and sub-plots of the Italian poem somewhat bewildering. At times he is willing to see this as a sign of Ariosto's great genius. Like an unskilful apprentice he can only concentrate on isolating one line:

> The historie all interlest I find
> Wyth syndrie sayings of so great delyt,
> That singlie most I from the rest out spind,
> As the unskilfull prentes imperfyt
> Quho fyns the gould frie from the laton quyt.
> No wonder thocht my wittis waver will
> In flowing feild of sic profound indyt.

At other times he is less flattering to his master, talking of his 'lairge prolixit histoir' and refusing to trace the future life of Angelica and Medoro on the curt grounds that the remaining material as told by Ariosto is 'imperfyt and tedius'.

Stewart, then, is not a passive imitator cowed by a work of genius. Rather is he intrigued by the original and wishes, through his invention, to produce his own version. Thus, although for the most part he translates quite closely, he is at the same time creating a new vision of the work. First of all 'as an apprentice' he does concentrate on one major character – Angelica, her own attitude to love and the effect love of her has on Christian and pagan heroes alike. The most extreme fall is that of Orlando, dragged down from being the major hope of Christianity to becoming the weeping, melancholy knight of Stewart's Canto IV. In Canto VI he is the deluded figure who follows an illusion of Angelica into Atlantes' castle. Finally madness sets in and he wreaks vengeance on nature and himself. Stewart, his own verse rhetorically capable of describing and commenting on the horror of this scene, assesses the extent of his fall:

> Thair bluid upsucking, quhairwith blubbrit beine
> His visage quhilk appeird so bawld befoir.
> Far mycht he now defigurat be seine
> From that renownit wordie chiftane keine,
> Umquhyle the beild and piller firm of France.

But, pathetic as the sight of Orlando's descent may be, Stewart is careful to let us see it as only one example of love's unanswerable power. By drawing together incidents from different parts of the *Orlando*, he shows us men of all creeds, stations and morals succumbing in turn to Angelica's charms. Nor does Stewart lose Ariosto's wit in describing their various fates. The proud Sacripanto is perfunctorily overthrown by Bradamante. The hyperserious Rinaldo is busily fighting for Angelica, while she is making good her escape. The lustful old hermit is described so that we condemn him and welcome the arrival of Ruggiero. But a few lines later young nobility is reacting just the same as ancient perversion:

Quho mycht refraine now for this ladie saik
To mont aloft with all his members tycht.

And so in the end it is only potential performance and not strict moral distinctions which divide the hermit and the pure knight!

Angelica, meanwhile, although lurching from one melodrama of near rape to another, does not come across very sympathetically. She may claim chastity as the highest principle in her life but the saving of her own skin is also undeniably important to her. She callously outwits even faithful friends like Sacripanto to save herself. She too must be taught that love rules and so the proud, chaste beauty, who has dismissed the finest knights on both sides at length falls for a shepherd boy having no merit bar his physical beauty:

The curling yellow hair upon his heed
Scho interteind with hir maist tender hand,
And stairing on his beutie quhyt and reed
All stupifact as statue dois scho stand.

Now most of this material does appear in the *Orlando*. The novelty of Stewart's treatment is due to three major alterations. The first is related to the overall form of the two works. By narrowing the focus and showing one man after another attempt to defeat Angelica's chastity, he makes a powerful and explicit comment on the universal power of love and lust, driving home his message with less subtlety but perhaps more direct moral force than in the original. For Stewart does not only isolate one strand, he places that strand within a much neater, analytic form, which encourages comparisons and contrasts to be drawn. At all times he is striving to impose a recognizable pattern on the events he has chosen to extrapolate from the *Orlando Furioso*. Thus Sacripanto's lament in Canto II is followed by Angelica's in Canto III and Orlando's in Canto IV. If the nymphs inspire Canto II, Melpomene is the force behind Canto IV, Ramnusia behind

Canto XI and Cleo for the last Canto of all. This briefer, more orderly approach allows him to make clearcut contrasts – the loyal Sacripanto against the despairing Rinaldo; the lust of the aged hermit against that of Ruggiero. Most obviously of all, Orlando and Angelica are contrasted and compared. Both fall through sins against God, one deserting the Christian cause, the other becoming proud. One conquers love after a long period of subjugation, the other is entrapped by love after disdaining it.

If Stewart's preference for explicitness over implicitness, the balance of symbolic instances over the lights and shadows of narrative and a rigid scheme over the more amorphous form of the *Orlando Furioso* shows how determined he is not to be thought a passive imitator, his second major alteration shows how anxious he is to be a loyal 'prentise' to James VI and the Castalian ideal. James held firmly to the belief that his own verse, and hopefully that of his followers, would be Christian. Essentially of course Ariosto's epic is a Christian tale. When Astolpho ascends into the heavens on Orlando's behalf the motivation is Christian and soon the pagan power is brought to an end. But Stewart with his many additional Biblical parallels and above all his final Canto XII relating everything to God's will shows once again his preference for direct statement. What was implicit in Astolpho's ascent is here explicitly related to the Boethian doctrine of greater good arising from misfortune:

> Bot our guid God quho rycht guvernis all
> Will weill delyver from maist deip distres:
> Quhen force and judgement of all men is small
> In onie wayis for to prepair redres,
> By expectation than his mycht expres
> Maist suddanlie dissolvith strongest snair.

There follow the Christian examples of Joseph, David and the people of Bethulia, all introduced by Stewart. It can thus be seen that those Cantos concerned with Orlando (I, IV, VI, VII, XI) lead inevitably to and are intended to illustrate this moral. Likewise it is God's will that Angelica should learn meekness through her passion for Medoro. So Stewart's poem has a double message – no man or woman of whatever quality may withstand love but no love may compare or compete with the love of God.

Scottish poets have a bit of a reputation for taking free-moving works of genius and giving them a more compact, almost allegorical form. But before you automatically presume that Stewart's 'Abbregement' must be the work of a neat but inferior intellect, let me remind you that in many ways his *Roland* is to the *Orlando* as Henryson's *Testament* is to Chaucer's *Troilus*. All in all, the non-Scots works are in each case probably superior but to the Scots in each case must go the credit for recasting part of the original material in such a fashion that the new poems have to be judged against different critical criteria, not as poor shadows of their begetters. And this leads naturally to the last major difference between the *Roland* and the *Orlando*. A self-conscious master of rhetoric, Stewart did not always abridge. In many instances, some comic, some of the highest seriousness, he expanded on his model. Choosing rhyming couplets rather than Ariosto's 'ottava rima', he created memorable passages of such vitality that M. P. McDiarmid rightly called the *Roland* 'the most brilliant and energetic poem of the brief Scots Renaissance'. In this instance, two examples may suffice. The first hilariously describes the hermit's fury at his impotence:

> He dammest drouppit doune againe as deid
> With panchie mouth als haw as onie leed,
> And all his hyd most lyk ane skrimplit ront;
> No chap nor chak mycht mak him lift his heed,
> His bruisit bit was worne so rustie blont;
> In vain he forst him to that flowing font,
> In vaine he schaiks the brydile to and fro,
> In vaine he wrocht for he wold nevir mont,
> And vainlie vaine he lang tormentit so,
> Quhill hir besyd at last he sleipit tho.

The second, making full use of Middle Scots' hard consonants and shorter vowel sounds, depicts Orlando's madness at its height:

> His hands outragius did his visage skart
> Maist horribile, and with ane hiddeus brall
> For raidge he roird and restles did dispart
> His scheild, his gantlat and his corslat tall;
> Heir fell the brassats, thair lyis Durandal,
> Strong nails he breaks, his cuissots aff did slyd;
> His helm, his gorget and his harneis all
> In thousand peicis he disparplit wyd.

Stewart's Roland will rightly never rank with its model as one of the greatest poems of all time. But he should be given credit for being one of the first Scots to adapt a major Italian work; for the thoroughness with which he employed his various sources; for the courage which decided not to attempt a timid translation but rather a creative re-working highlighting the powers of temporal and heavenly love and, not least, for understanding that it was pointless to try and recreate the lyrical beauty of Italian in Middle Scots and opting instead to use the rhetorical strengths of his own language to give energy and vitality to the tale.

¶ William Fowler, Secretary to Queen Anne and close friend of the King, is the other major Castalian, whose works owe much to Italian inspiration. Although not so skilful a craftsman as Stewart, he was better versed in the Italian language and to him especially must go the credit for making Italian writing well known in Jacobean Scotland. The three works which most concern us are his translations of Petrarch's *Trionfi* and Macchiavelli's *Il Principe* as well as his sonnet sequence, *The Tarantula of Love*.

Of these *The Triumphs* must surely be regarded as the least successful. Petrarch's work was already known in Scotland. James had a copy of it in his library, transferred there from Mary's. The Holyrood Shrovetide Masque of 1564 had been based on incidents from the poem and Rizzio is known to have taken a prominent part. Fowler in his Preface of 1587 confesses not only an admiration for the original but a contempt for earlier 'French and Inglish traductionis', which have 'magled and in everie member miserablie maimed and dismembered' it, showing once again the thoroughness with which Castalians approached the task of translation.

Unfortunately, Fowler can scarcely claim to have improved on the efforts of Morley, de la Forge and d'Opède. He was using a text round the borders of which were mythological and classical parallels to the events told in the poem. In part, presumably, to permit him to incorporate some of these, Fowler decided to use couplets of iambic heptameter instead of the shorter line favoured by Petrarch. This meant that he was forced to expand on the original material. At times his rhetorical skills proved adequate for the task. There are many excellent parallel constructions on the Hebraic model, while native word is often set next to classical equivalent in the fashion of Caxton. But more often the longer line results in near meaningless additions whose only function is to eke out the metre. Petrarch writes:

> Era sì pieno il cor di meraviglie
> Ch'i' stava come l'uom che non po dire.
> [So full of amazement was my heart
> That I stood like a man who cannot speak.]

This becomes for Fowler:

> So muche my hart wes then amaised, so much of mervell full
> That I thair stoode, even as a man that stupid stands
>   and dull.

Sometimes lengthy classical parallels are drawn in from the margins of the text he was consulting, further slowing down the vitality of the argument. At others he infuriatingly condescends to his audience by stating baldly what they had already imaginatively grasped. Seeing Jove chained to the Chariot of Love, Petrarch makes no comment but Fowler fatuously confides to us that this shows the God 'Subdewed by Love and led by love to mak his pompe more fair'. Like Stewart too, he is extremely keen to stress the final Christian message so that the dignified opening twelve lines of the 'Trionfo dell'Eternità' expressing the poet's sense of guilt and delay in opening himself to grace is translated in 26 much longer lines, heavy with stylistic reduplications and embarrassing breast-beatings.

Fowler had admired the *Trionfi* for its 'statelye verse', its 'morall sentences', 'propper and pithie arguments' and 'golden freinyeis of Eloquence'. Unfortunately, like many Castalians he believed in the piling of ornamentation on ornamentation. So, although he did Scots a practical service by translating this influential work into their own tongue, it is doubtful whether he could be said to have done them a 'literary' service. The 'statelye verse' he made longwinded and aureate. His chosen heptameters enabled him to explain the 'morall sentences' at excruciating length, to expand interminably on the 'goodlye sayings', make the 'propper and pithie arguments' tedious in their longwindedness and, above all, to elaborate on the 'golden freinyeis of Eloquence' though sometimes with scant regard for the more precise rules of grammar.

By comparison his translation of *Il Principe* can fairly be termed an outstanding success. The first extended piece of Italian prose to be turned into Scots, it received a careful and accurate treatment from Fowler. The political situation at the time gives us some hints as to why this should be so. James VI was, in the 1590s, at work on his treatise on kingship, *Basilicon Doron*. The evidence suggests that Fowler's work on *Il Principe* was intended in part to aid his prince. Certainly it is notable that the only Chapters omitted from his version are those whose contents would have annoyed James. Chapters 5 to 8 with their emphasis on conquest would have been anathema to James the peace-lover; and Chapter 9's discussion of a citizen prince would have sounded almost like blasphemy to a staunch believer in Divine Right. What James wanted was, above all, an accurate version of Macchiavelli's ideas, not interspersed with flights of imagination deriving from the mind of his wife's secretary. In this instance politics came before art.

Fowler provided just this – a careful, even sympathetic, translation. His love of elaboration, however, could not entirely be suppressed, especially as Macchiavelli's style was in itself simpler than the flowing Isocratean periods then favoured for Scottish prose. But, almost without exception, Fowler confined himself to embellishments, which, though they might render the original more vivid, in no way blurred the central idea. A comparison from Chapter 25 between Macchiavelli's account of Fortune's activities and Fowler's may illustrate the point.

> E assomiglio quella a uno di questi fiumi rovinosi, che quando s'adirano, allagano e' piani, ruinano li alberi e li edifizii, lievano da questa parte terreno, pongono da quell' altra: ciascuno fugge loro dinanzi, ognuno cede allo impeto loro, sanza potervi in alcuna parte obstare.

> [And I compare her to one of those torrential rivers which when they rage, flood the plains, destroy trees and buildings, lift up earth from one part and lay it in another: everyone flees before them, everybody yields to their fury, unable to oppose them in any way.]

> FOWLER. For I compair fortoun to a violent flood, rining from the montains with impetuositie and ravishment, that whils as he is swillted and deborded, overfloweth all the plane, drowneth the nighbour banks, violentlye plucketh up the treis, and turneth away the houses and forceablye caryeis and transporteth and heapeth an part of earth til another ground, and so all pepill, giving place til his furie, flyeth far off, having no meanes to withstand it.

Fowler adds visual details such as the mountain; he shows a preference for intensifying adverbs, for the strengthening of one verb by another close in meaning and his overall syntax is more obviously Latinate than Macchiavelli's. But his departures are in inessentials. His overall message is the same as Macchiavelli's and he certainly finds prose a much more conducive medium for translation than he had the heptameters of the *Triumphs*.

Before discussing his Sonnet Sequence, *The Tarantula of Love*, it is important to note the influence of James on Fowler's writing. A courtier, dependent on Royal favour, Fowler was unlikely to try and annoy his monarch. Nor did he! *The Triumphs* were written as part of James's directive to translate influential European classics; *The Prince* was begun in order to aid James's *Basilicon Doron* and now a series of sonnets appears in accordance with James's idea that a distinctively *Scottish* sonnet should be the linch-pin of his poetic renaissance.

But the title and the very first sonnet indicate that *The Tarantula* is in one important sense going to be different from James's *Amatoria*, Stewart's *Rapsodies* and the sonnets of Montgomerie.

Each of these contributions had been primarily French in inspiration. Du Bartas, Desportes, Saint Gelais, Ronsard – these were the poets to whom the other Castalians most readily turned. By calling his sequence by the apparently unlikely name of 'Tarantula', Fowler signified that he was continuing his bias towards Italian sources. It is in Castiglione's *Il Cortegiano* that we are told that the tarantula's bite leads to the madnesses of verse, music and love. Nor is this all that Fowler takes from *Il Cortegiano*. As the poet lover moves slowly from lust to love through the enduring of a parting and a growing preference for the idea of beauty rather than one particular woman, he is slowly climbing that ladder of love outlined in Book 4 by Bembo. In the end, as Bembo had counselled, he decides to transfer his love from Lady to God, thus reaching the highest rung. It is therefore on a religious note that *The Tarantula* ends:

> As I IN ONE GOD EVER ay haith trust,
> So ar his promeis steadfast, trew and just.

If any doubts remained that this was the first truly Italianate Sonnet sequence in Scots, they would be demolished by the very first sonnet in the sequence with its clear echoing of 'Voi ch'ascoltate in rime sparse il suono', the opening sonnet in Petrarch's *Rime*:

> O you who heres the accents of my smart
> Diffus'd in ryme and sad disordered verse,
> Gif ever flams of love hath toutcht youre hart,
> I trust with sobbs and teares the same to perse. . . .

Throughout the 75 sonnets which make up the sequence the voices not only of Petrarch, but of Rota, Sannazaro and Boiardo can also be heard. It was only after the Union of the Crowns that Scotland began to welcome Italian literature as generously as the English had done in the previous generation but Fowler and Stewart had both done much to lay the foundations on which writers like Drummond could build.

Although much has been made of Fowler's unevenness as a writer, one sonnet in particular (TAR 22) gives the lie to those who claim he was incapable of truly great writing. Based on Petrarch's 'Or che'l ciel e la terra e'l vento tace', it presents a striking portrait of all nature sinking to rest, while the poet alone wrestles with love's torments:

> The day is done, the sunn dothe ells declyne,
> Night now approaches and the moone appeares,
> The twinkling starrs in firmament dois schyne,
> Decoring with the poolles there circled spheres.
> The birds to nests, wyld beasts to denns reteirs,

The moving leafes unmoved now repose,
Dewe dropps dois fall, the portraicts of my teares.
The waves within the seas theme calmlye close,
To all things nature ordour dois impose,
Bot not to love that proudlye dothe me thrall,
Quha all the dayes and night, but chainge or choyse,
Steirs up the coales of fyre unto my fall,
And saves his breirs and thornes within my hart,
The fruits quhairoff ar doole, greiff, grones and smart.

This famous Petrarchan sonnet has been translated many times, but few of the versions can match the simplicity and the rhetorical skill of Fowler's poem.

Thus, if Fowler's major importance was a historical one – being the major 'Italian' voice at a predominantly 'French' court – and if some of his verse is perhaps best forgotten he may justly be proud of some of his Italian-influenced sonnets and of his major prose translation. The legacy he passed on to his nephew Drummond was not inconsiderable and was certainly thus valued by the younger poet.

¶ Drummond himself is, inevitably, our next principal concern. Arguably, no Scot before or since has been so deeply immersed in Italian literature or been able to imitate it so brilliantly, while maintaining that recognisable originality of invention so highly valued by James VI. After 1603, when James and many of his Castalian band had moved south; when the deserted court of Edinburgh stood at the heart of a country which in many ways now resembled a cultural desert, Drummond remained in his estates at Hawthornden and was recognised by Scots both at home and in London as an important writer and man of culture. The fact that many of the Castalian ideals had ended – that Scots increasingly wrote in English and that Italian sources were now as popular as French, suited the young landowner with his vast linguistic repertoire and his sensitive control over the 'southern tongue'.

On the other hand he experienced and did not relish that sense of isolation felt by so many stay-at-home Scots, often envying his friends William Alexander and Robert Ayton for their ability, in London, to mix with English literati like Jonson and Drayton. For at this time national feelings were subsidiary to literary alliances. Drummond was a Petrarchan or a Spenserean, a friend of Drayton with William Alexander his major Scottish ally. Against them stood the metaphysicals, ranged behind Donne and Jonson, with Robert Ayton and Alexander Craig the best known Scots.

Even in a short study of this sort it is necessary to preface our detailed study of Drummond with proof that he did not stand alone in his love for Italian literature. The widely read Sir William Alexander has echoes from Petrarch, Tasso and others in his lyric sequence *Aurora*. Indeed Tasso's themes and techniques in particular appealed to him so much that it comes as no surprise to read in his critical work, the *Anacrisis*, after assessments of Virgil, Ovid, Horace and Statius, that, 'There is no man doth satisfy me more than that notable Italian, Torquato Tasso, in whom I find no blemish but that he doth make Solyman, by whose overthrow he would grace Rinaldo, to die fearfully, belying the part that he would have personated during his life.' A fellow 'Spenserean', David Murray, turned rather to Trissino, re-working his *Sofonisba* in *Sophonisba*, and devoting a sonnet to Bellizarius, Lieutenant to Emperor Justinian and one of the heroes of Trissino's *L'Italia Liberata da' Goti*.

Nor were the Scottish 'metaphysicals' to be outdone. Alexander Craig may not have attempted close imitations from the Italian but in *The Amorose Songes* he celebrated eight different mistresses, each representing a different attitude to love. Not surprisingly the pure, chaste Erantina is based on a well-known Italian model: she is the re-incarnation of Petrarch's Laura:

> Sweete lovely Laura, modest, chast, and cleene,
> It seemes that Poet Petrarche tooke delight,
> Thy spotles prayse in daintie lines to dight,
> By Prophecies, before thy selfe was seene.

And although the poems dealing with her in no instance suggest direct imitation, her attitudes and the imagery used to convey them prove Craig at the very least to be well versed in the Petrarchan conventions. Sir Robert Ayton on the other hand does both imitate and translate from Italian, showing a particular interest in the pastoral mode. Certainly the following lines from Ayton's 'Faire cruell Silvia' might cause students of Guarini to wonder if they had not met a similar argument before:

> Faire cruell Silvia, since thou scornes my teares
> And over lookes my cares with careless Eye,
> Since my request in love offends thy eares,
> Hence forth I vow to hold my peace and dye.
> But while I hold my peace, those things shall cry,
> The brookes shall murmur and the winds complaine,
> The hills, the dales, the deserts where I lye
> With echoes of my sighes shall preach my paine.

It is the first octet of a sonnet, the whole of which is closely based on part of Act 1 Scene 2 of *Il Pastor Fido*. Ayton changes the heroine's name to one more easily assimilated into English metre; he also alters the order of the mourners but generally keeps close to the theme of the original. The equivalent passage in the Italian reads:

Cruda Amarilli, che col nome ancora,
D'amar, ahi lasso, amaramente insegni!
Amarilli, del candido ligustro
Più candida e più bella,
Ma de l'àspido sordo
E più sorda e più fèra e più fugace,
Poi che col dir t'offendo,
I' mi morrò tacendo;
Ma grideran per me le piagge e i monti
E questa selva, a cui
Sì spesso il tuo bel nome
Di risonare insegno.

[Cruel Amarillis, alas your very name still encourages my unhappy love. Amarillis, fairer and more beautiful than white privet but deafer and wilder and more fleeting than the pitiless viper, since my words offend you I will die in silence; but for me there will be cries of lament from the hills, the mountains, and this wood which I have so often taught to echo your name.]

Drummond's particular genius thus reached its fulfilment at a time when many external forces seemed inimical to Scots writing but when interest in Italian authors was on the increase.

Drummond's situation of course proved ideal for moulding a thoughtful, erudite and imitative poet. Born in 1585, the son of a minor courtier, he attended Edinburgh University, graduating MA in 1605. He went abroad for a spell, studying law at the University of Bourges. But when his father died in 1610, he settled down in his estate at Hawthornden. There, despite having all the duties incumbent on a laird, he also had plenty of time to improve his knowledge of various European languages and to read widely. It proved time well spent, although many critics, like Ben Jonson, feared it produced an outdated, overly imitative type of verse.

I shall begin my analysis of Drummond by putting both of these criticisms in their context. First of all was Drummond behind his time? Jonson was surprised to find him still adhering to Petrarch and Italian verse, when in England French sources were now preferred. True, if Drummond had been an English poet he would have been rather démodé. But he was a Castalian and in Scotland the source preferences had been different – a preference for French writing before the Union and a preference for Italian writing only after it. Secondly, if Jonson had cared to examine in particular Drummond's adaptations of Petrarch, he would have found that most of them are very free, proving Drummond to be aware that this poet was now so well known that close imitation was unnecessary. And that is why both in sheer volume and in closeness of imitation, he prefers Petrarch's successor Tasso and Tasso's successor Marino. Before casually dismissing Drummond, it is necessary first to be aware of important differences between the Scottish and English poetic traditions and then to analyse carefully the authors he chooses to imitate and the manner of those imitations. As I have demonstrated elsewhere, such a study shows Drummond very much alive to the latest movements in Italian literature and to be at no time a servile translator.

Jonson's second criticism, that Drummond's work smelled too much of the schools – that is, that it showed too heavy a reliance on past authors and on rhetorical handbooks – is on the face of things, incontrovertible. Drummond is an expert, though a very subtle, rhetorician. Also a high percentage of his work derives in some way or other from earlier writers. He does show a preference for Italians, but French, English, Spanish and Portuguese also figure. It is therefore impossible to shield him from Jonson's prime objection – that he is not a metaphysical, composing original verse, shocking his readers into attention by daring use of the conceit. But it is more than possible, it is *necessary*, to demonstrate that, far from being some sort of literary chamaeleon, Drummond never lost integrity in the sense of sacrificing his own ideas at the altars of the poems he was adapting. Imitation, King James had advocated, but Imitation controlled by Invention. The idea is older than Quintilian and was held in Classical, Mediaeval and Renaissance times to be the highest type of art. Of all the Castalians, Drummond, with his careful adaptations, now remaining close to their originals, now departing from them, proves the master craftsman.

The most convenient way of proving this is to begin by isolating those ideas, which, from his works in prose as well as verse, fact as well as fiction, we know to be nearest to the poet's own heart. These include his fear of Time as a decaying force; his battles with the problem of Death; his belief in the recuperative powers of solitary thought and existence and his somewhat wavering but never abandoned Christian faith. And to begin with it is clear that when seeking poems to imitate for inclusion in the *Poems* or the *Flowres of Sion*, those which deal with these or related topics are most frequently selected. Drummond knows the overall philosophical framework of the sequences in advance and chooses in accordance with that overall plan. Thus he will seize on a single poem by a relatively unknown poet, if it strengthens an idea which he already holds. He opts for Valerio Belli's competent but scarcely brilliant madrigal on Death because it has a part to play in the overall pattern of the sequence:

> Questo mondo è una caccia, è cacciatrice
> La Morte vincitrice:
> I veltri suoi rapaci
> Sono cure mordaci,
> E morbi, e mal, da cui cacciati siamo:
> E se talhor fuggiamo,
> Vecchiezza sua compagna,
> Ci prende ne la ragna.
> [This world is a hunting place, the hunter victorious Death: her greedy hounds are pressing cares, disease and woe, by whom we are pursued. And if sometimes we do escape, Old Age, her companion, catches us in the net.]

This becomes Drummond's 'This world a Hunting is'. The imitation is very close but even here there are subtle changes. Drummond seems to find Belli's vision rather too clearcut. By introducing mythological figures such as Nimrod into his version; by bringing all the personified ills together and so emphasising them and by ending with a much more horrific vision of death, Drummond subtly moves the poem closer to his own philosophy.

> This world a Hunting is,
> The pray poore Man, the Nimrod fierce is Death,
> His speedie Grei-hounds are,
> Lust, sicknesse, Envie, Care,
> Strife that neere falles amisse,
> With all those ills which haunt us while we breath.
> Now, if (by chance) wee flie
> Of these the eager Chase,
> Old Age with stealing Pace,
> Castes up his nets, and there wee panting die.

These changes may seem slight but Drummond has substituted his own more gently melancholic tone for the clearcut propositions of the original. He has extended the didactic element in the poem and of course he has, in the last line, created a much more frightening, vivid picture of death than any achieved by Belli. In short, he has seized on this poem because its central theme appeals to him. He has 'imitated' in such a way that his own views at points replace the Italian's and then he has placed the new artefact in a sequence, *The Flowres of Sion,* where methodically he is using Christian teachings to combat those very fears of death and transience. He sees a purpose for it, once amended, within the particular arguments advanced in *The Flowres.*

Other more striking instances exist. Bembo, a poet from whom Drummond seldom borrows, provides in 'Lieta e chiusa contrada; ov'io m'involo' the model for 'Deare wood, and you sweet solitarie place'. The choice is again a thematic one – the values of solitude. But it is noticeable that Drummond omits the quasi-religious powers granted by Bembo to the solitary place in the second quatrain, preferring to develop the simpler idea of contentment suggested at the start and finish of the octet. Even in the sestet, where he returns to a closer adaptation, he tones down Bembo's relief at being released from all care into a simpler joy at escaping briefly from the stresses of the outside world. For Bembo the grove cures his problems; for Drummond it provides a better setting for reassessing them.

Having hopefully established Drummond as a sensitive follower of the doctrine of Imitation and Invention rather than a pedant with much linguistic skill but not an original thought in his head; having suggested that both the *Poems* and *Flowres of Sion* have carefully constructed and consistent arguments, only possible if his chosen sources were, in various ways, subjugated to Drummond's controlling vision, it may now be possible to look in more detail at the poet's particular interest in the work of his contemporary, Marino, who provides more 'sources' than any other Italian writer.

Thematically the reason for this is clear. Almost all of Drummond's obsessions are shared by Marino. The Italian's concern with death produced 'Fabro dela mia morte' which lies behind Drummond's 'A Dedale of my Death'. This soon links with the problem of mutability in 'Alma gentil, ch'anzi gran tempo l'ale', which inspires 'Sweet Soule, which in the Aprill of thy Yeares', just as 'O d'humano splendor breve baleno' instigates 'Of mortall Glorie o soone darkned Raye'. But it is certain that above all else, Drummond, the doubting Christian, anxious finally to allay his fears through Biblical faith, found Marino's Biblical lyrics of particular use in framing the *Flowres of Sion* with its intense battle between belief and unbelief.

Often Drummond remains very close to his model in these instances and the nativity scene drawn in 'For the Nativitie of our Lord' closely follows Marino's 'Felice notte, ond' a noi nasce il giorno' with only minor alterations in order and imagery. Compare too the opening quatrains of their prodigal son sonnets:

Cangia contrada, e 'n procurar diletto
Altronde, unqua non hebbi altro ch'affanno,
Volgendo in signoria d'empio Tiranno
I dolci imperi del paterno affetto.

[I changed country, but in the pursuit of pleasure elsewhere
I never found anything but torment, exchanging the gentle
commands of my father's affection for the rule of a cruel
Tyrant.]

I Countries chang'd new pleasures out to finde,
But Ah! for pleasure new I found new paine,
Enchanting pleasure so did Reason blind,
That Fathers love and wordes I scorn'd as vaine.

But when his religious beliefs meet poetic opposition, Drummond will depart as readily from Marino as he would from Belli
or Petrarch. A good example occurs in the second quatrain of
'Beneath a sable vaile'. Depicting the man who aspires to more
knowledge of supernatural truths, Drummond comments:

Through those thicke mistes when any mortall wight
Aspires with halting pace and eyes that weepe,
To pore, and in his Misteries to creepe
With thunders hee and Lightnings blastes their sight.

This sympathy for the poor, struggling human is in part sympathy
for Drummond himself, his delving into metaphysical questions
and his intensely experienced sense of inadequacy. It also marks
a sudden deviation from his model. At the equivalent point
Marino had stressed the overweening rashness of such inquirers:

E s'altri spia per queste nebbie immonde
I suoi giudici in nero velo avolti,
Gli humani ingegni temerari, e stolti,
Col lampo abbaglia, e col suo tuon confonde.

[And if anyone spies through these gloomy mists His dark-
veiled judgments, He blinds our rash and foolish human
intelligence with lightning, and confounds it with His thun-
der.]

Here is the art of the eclectic borrower neatly summed up.
Attracted by Marino's skill and the overall theme of a poem
dealing with God's apparent concealment from striving man,
Drummond inserts it into a sequence dealing with just this
problem but also containing adaptations from poets as varied as
Petrarch and Du Bellay, Desportes and Guglia. Moreover, on
the one major point at which Marino's thought conflicts with the
message of the sequence, Drummond's invention steps in to
restore overall thematic consistency.

Stylistically, too, the poets are very close, sharing in particular the same rhetorical preferences. My researches on Drummond and those of Mirollo on Marino highlight an interest in similar techniques – notably parenthesis, inversion and apostrophe – but within the framework of a thorough versing in all rhetorical skills. They both delight in building up a firm rhetorical structure heavily dependent on techniques of symmetry such as parallel words and clauses; chiasmus and doubling. In short, the basis of Marino's style, like Drummond's, is a tension between a neat, almost neoclassical rhetorical balance and the more sonorous rhythms of classical verse. It is this mixture, allied to the more musical devices of onomatopoeia, alliteration and assonance, which provides a medium at once controlled and flowing, at once incisive and harmonious.

But closeness does not imply identity. Marino is much more attracted to daring metaphysical conceits than Drummond and so in the end their verse for all its thematic and rhetorical similarities does not make the same overall impression. Nor, I am sure, would Drummond have wished that. As Marino shocks us through his ingenuity, Drummond teaches very similar lessons in a quieter, more melancholic but every bit as skilful manner. I therefore conclude this part of the discussion with a sonnet, which seems to me to encapsulate some of these skills. And I do this because I am sure that Drummond's true worth will only at last be realised when comparative critics, having discussed his many debts admit that the final voice is unique and worth listening to in and for itself. There is a minor debt to Passerat in the opening quatrain but that is all.

> I know that all beneath the moone decayes,
> And what by mortalles in this world is brought,
> In Times great periods shall returne to nought,
> That fairest states have fatall nights and dayes:
> I know how all the Muses heavenly layes,
> With toyle of spright which are so dearly bought,
> As idle sounds of few or none are sought
> And that nought lighter is than airie praise.
> I know fraile beautie like the purple flowre,
> To which one morne oft birth and death affords,
> That love a jarring is of mindes accords,
> Where sense and will invassall reasons power:
>   Know what I list, this all can not mee move,
>   But that (o mee!) I both must write and love.

It is particularly fitting to end this section of the study with the gently melancholy philosophy of Drummond, his perfect ear for rhythm and his ability to bring rhetorical skills to bear on his work without turning them into manneristic exercises. For Drummond represents the zenith of that first Renaissance in Scottish letters, when authors here looked outwards as well as inwards for inspiration and outwards especially to Italy. I have isolated Stewart, Fowler and Drummond but have mentioned more whose work was immeasurably enriched through acquaintance with Dante, Petrarch, Ariosto, Tasso, Marino and others. This is a situation to which I believe we are returning in the twentieth century. But from the mid-seventeenth century till now is a long time and it is first necessary to look at the intervening years, considering not only the many great Scottish writers who maintained links with Italy but also some of the forces inimical to that alliance.

III

The Eighteenth and Nineteenth Centuries

Poetically, of course, the eighteenth century in Scotland is the age of the vernacular revival and Burns. Increasingly the followers of this movement reacted against the mannerised, imitative and largely anglicised verse of Drummond and his fellows. Folk traditions were revered, native culture aggressively held to be superior to foreign and the Scots vernacular preferred to English. As this line hardened in the nineteenth century with the cult of Burnsian imitation and the Whistle Binkie volumes, as well as the 'kailyard' tendencies in novel and drama, there can be little doubt that one very important movement was in broad terms antipathetic to the sort of Italianate verse studied in the preceding section. It is important however, to place this evidence within its fuller context. Otherwise it might appear that Scottish-Italian literary relationships came to a full stop at this time; something which self-evidently is not the case.

If we look at the wider cultural scene at this time, we find foreign influences stronger than ever. The popularity of the Grand Tour was at its height and we find Boswell, for example, enjoying a prolonged stay in Italy, centred on Turin, Rome, Florence and Siena, followed by his famous visit to Corsica. There he avidly read the *Orlando Furioso,* using amorous quotations from it in his letters, with a view to furthering his own love conquests. David Hume spent two years in Italy. Like Boswell he appears to have read widely, telling Adam Smith that he is about to begin Boiardo's *Orlando Innamorato* and feeling qualified to generalise on the state of Italian romance and prose. Smith himself writes even more widely on Italian subjects, now preferring Macchiavelli as a historian to Guicciardini; now embarking on a profound analysis of the strengths and weaknesses of Italian comedy; now discussing the major linguistic differences between English and Italian.

At the same time Scottish painters often went to Italy to finish their training; Edinburgh singing was dominated by the formidable Signora Doria and Signora Corri as well as the tenor Tenducci. The studying of foreign languages under accredited teachers became more and more a hobby of the intelligentsia. Undeniably it was the very force of this cosmopolitanism, which eventually led some Scots to feel their sense of national identity being threatened. But if it was this understandable emotion

[22]

which largely gave the Vernacular revival its continued momentum, even here some distinctions have to be made. And the first is to contrast the example and attitudes of its begetter, Allan Ramsay, with those of his more famous successors Fergusson and Burns. Ramsay sees positive signs in the literary climate of the early eighteenth century in Scotland. For him, there was no opposition between vernacular writing and the imitative tradition of Drummond. Rather he saw the one movement enriching the other. His attitude to Imitation and Invention is very close to that of James VI and in his *Fables* at least he consciously composes in a European genre, aware of indirect debts to French and Italian sources.

What has to be remembered is that, for a generation after Ramsay's death, the revival wavered and as it wavered the grip of foreign cultures on Scotland became tighter. Thus, when Fergusson and later Burns took up their predecessor's challenge, they did so at a time when Ramsay's vision of Scottish and European fruitfully co-existing had become threatened. To establish one's Scottishness, one had in part to decry foreign culture, traditions, even food. Thus Burns does not merely say, a Scot should eat haggis. He is also quite clear on what he should not eat!

> Is there that owre his French *ragout*,
> Or *olio* that wad staw a sow
> Or *fricassée* wad mak her spew
> Wi' perfect sconner,
> Looks down wi' sneering, scornfu' view
> On sic a dinner.

He is opposing that group of 'fops' who automatically condescended to all things Scottish and elevated things foreign. Ramsay had earlier noted their presence but put his faith in Scottish common sense overcoming their excesses. Time had sadly proved him wrong. We know from the literary interests of both Fergusson and Burns that they valued French, Spanish and Italian writings. But as *dramatic* poets at a time when they felt the voice of Scotland should specifically make itself heard, they naturally adopted a rigorously national persona. Thus Fergusson, who was both a friend of and collaborator with Tenducci, feels able to satirise him in 'The Canongate Playhouse' and to condemn his Italian songs as 'a bastard breed' in the 'Elegy on the Death of Scots Music'.

Not surprisingly a search for Italian influences in the work of these two great poets proves a rather sterile endeavour. True, in a letter to Alexander Cunningham, Burns states that he 'translated a verse of an Italian song' for Urbani. This is the, usually omitted, opening verse of 'Stay, my charmer'. It reads:

Feel, oh, feel my bosom beating
As the busy moments fleeting,
Pit-a-patty still repeating,
Like the little mallet's blow.

The original is unknown to me but it is clearly after the style of Metastasio. Anticipations are also raised when we compare the opening stanza of 'Behold the hour, the boat arrive!' a lyric sent to Clarinda in 1791 with Metastasio's *La Partenza* and the stanza beginning, 'Ecco qual fiero istante'. They are indeed close but research discloses an English intermediary by Father David Dalrymple, a Scots version of which appeared in the *Edinburgh Magazine* of 1774. This last seems the most likely source for Burns's lyric, being consistent with his interest in refurbishing Scots songs.

The vernacular revolution therefore arose at a time when Scotland's links with Europe were particularly strong; its earliest practitioner saw it as a complement to the imitative tradition of Drummond and even Burns and Fergusson adopted exaggeratedly chauvinistic personae in their verse, necessary for their artistic rôle as they conceived it but to some degree contradicted by their catholic interest in European classics. To all this we must add one final and very important piece of evidence. Although the quality of Burns's verse in particular has rightly led critics to see the movement of which he was the zenith as the crucial one in Scots poetry at this time, in terms of overall output it was still a minor movement. Both general Petrarchan imitation and the more precise techniques of translation and adaptation continued unabated. True, this tradition showed every sign of having exhausted its potential; true, it produced some excruciatingly bad verse – but the literati in general continued to prefer it as being more in line with their ideal of a European family of nations. Also in writers like William Hamilton of Bangour and Dr Alexander Pennecuick it could boast practitioners, who if not inspired were at least proficient 'makars'.

Hamilton belonged to a prosperous country family, spent some time in Europe, was very well educated and, like Drummond, inherited estates. He therefore had the leisure to read widely and indulge his interest in poetry. A contemporary of Ramsay, he co-operated with that poet although their attitudes to art were quite different. On working relationships such as this were based the hopes for an all-embracing and powerful Scottish poetic movement, capable of including Hamilton's Petrarchan, English poems as well as Ramsay's Scots satires.

Hamilton's close poetic imitations come from classical authors, including Pindar, Anacreon, Virgil and Horace. When he refers to 'Italy, the blest indulgent land, the muse's best beloved', he is almost certainly thinking mainly of classical authors. Yet he knows Petrarch's work, either in the original or in translation:

Smote by a simple village maid,
See noble Petrarch night and day
Pour his soft sorrows thro' the shade.

Frequently he calls his imaginary and chaste mistress, Laura:

Yet were thy cheek as Venus fair;
Bloom'd all the Paphian goddess there,
Such as she bless'd Adonis' arms;
Thou couldst but equal LAURA's charms.

Over and over again Petrarchan conceits appear in his verse, most notably in 'Palinode', 'Upon hearing his Picture was in a Lady's breast' and 'You ask me, charming fair'. There also seem to be structural and particular parallels between the *Trionfi* and his long, rather stilted work, *Contemplations*.

Dr Alexander Pennecuick preferred to continue the closer line of adaptation and translation favoured at James VI's court. Little is known of his life except that he inherited the estate of Newhall and was a master of many languages including Italian. The overall standard of his writing is such that it does not warrant extended treatment. Suffice it to say, that like Ayton, he was primarily attracted to the work of Guarini, even adapting the same speech by Amarilli in Act 2 of *Il Pastor Fido*, ('Care selve beate') as his predecessor. Here he remains reasonably close to the text, whereas in 'O Mirtil, best of Sheepherds', (whose source is also part of *Il Pastor Fido*) he adapts with great freedom the order and indeed the nature of Amarilli's argument in 'O Mirtillo, Mirtillo, anima mia'. Finally his rendering of Macchiavelli's *Belfagor*, while generally faithful, does aim at simplifying the original and at playing down its didactic aims. He highlights the wit and the raciness of the fable itself and if the final product is neither so profound nor so moral as Macchiavelli's tale, Pennecuick's version is nonetheless an enjoyably humorous story and one of the few pieces of well-written English prose composed by Scotsmen at this time.

Although the work of both Hamilton and Pennecuick can at times be both interesting and skilful, it does represent the end of a tradition, begun in the 1580s and now in a decadent phase. It will therefore come as no surprise that the three major Scottish poets of the eighteenth and nineteenth centuries, whose writing shows evidence of Italian influence, express this influence in new and more creative manners. James Thomson, for example, won praise from both Burns and Hamilton. This ability to impress poets on both sides of the divide was in part due to his language. Although he uses English throughout as a medium, his style, as Nichol Smith has argued, owes much to the consciously rhetorical and Latinate tradition in writing so strongly fostered in Scotland. Burns too saw him as one of the first Scots to react against classicism in verse and turn to direct observation of nature. As a result he often echoes Thomson's *Seasons,* most notably in 'Now westlin winds and slaught'ring guns', 'A Winter Night' and 'Mary Morison'. Lord Byron to a large degree stood apart from the literary conflicts within Scotland but his admiration for Burns and his connections with the English Romantic movement show where his sympathies lay. His exile in Italy and his whole upbringing, however, guaranteed that he would not ally himself with the Vernacular Revolution but express his own complex personality in English verse, which at times relied heavily on Italian sources. The second James Thomson, writing in the latter half of the nineteenth century, belongs to a period when the tensions we have been discussing were fast becoming memories. In addition, his acutely melancholic personality at once results in his poetry being so forcefully pessimistic as to defy classification and in his turning to a more modern Italian source, the equally pessimistic figure of Leopardi. I shall now examine the contribution of these three writers in turn.

¶ The first James Thomson, whose *Seasons* and verses on Sir Isaac Newton both exerted influence on Italian writers, had visited Italy and spoke the language fluently. Italian influence on his work is of two distinct kinds. There is first of all the influence of Italy and its culture, particularly as expressed in *Liberty.* Given the title and Thomson's idealistic classical yearnings ('I long to see the fields whence Virgil gathered his immortal honey'), it is not surprising that modern Italy comes in for harsh criticism. Contrasted unfavourably with the example both of classical Italy and of modern Britain, it emerges as an example of lost greatness, of oppression and poverty. In a particularly contrived passage in Part 1, the poet moves from a contrast between the past's 'exulting states' and the present's 'dejected towns' to call dramatically on Oppression, now apparently the land's sole ruler:

> Come! by whatever sacred name disguised,
> Oppression come! and in thy works rejoice!
> See nature's richest plains to putrid fens

Turned by thy fury. From their cheerful bounds,
See razed the enlivening village, farm and seat.

Thomson also links Italy's loss of liberty with literary decadence, suggesting that a free Britain is beginning to show the way artistically to the land which first nurtured the Renaissance. This attitude was quite widely held and is another reason for Italian influence not being so powerful in this period.

Particular literary influences do, however, exist in his own verse. Some are slight. One feels, for example, that if Petrarch had not written 'Amor, Fortuna e la mia mente schiva', then Thomson's 'For ever Fortune wilt thou prove' could not have existed in its present form. Likewise, although his *Sophonisba* is not influenced directly by Trissino's famous tragedy, at least Thomson in the 'Prologue' shows awareness of the long tradition within which he is working:

With her th'Italian scene first learnt to glow;
And the first tears for her were taught to flow.

But it is *The Castle of Indolence* which shows the greatest debt to Italian writing and specifically to Tasso's *Gerusalemme Liberata*. Although Spenser's *Faerie Queene* is an even stronger influence, there are numerous instances where Tasso's version provides a closer parallel than Spenser's. Even MacKillop, whose bias is towards the English poet, prefers the Italian version of the feast as a source in Book I:

And every-where huge covered tables stood,
With wines high-flavour'd and rich viands crowned;
Whatever sprightly juice or tastful food,
On the green bosom of this Earth are found,
And all old Ocean genders in his round –
Some hand unseen These silently displayed,
Even undemanded by a sign or sound;
You need but wish, and, instantly obeyed,
Fair-ranged the dishes rose, and thick the glasses played.
(I.xxxiv)

Apprestar su l'erbetta, ov'è più densa
L'ombra, e vicino al suon de l'acque chiare,
Fece di sculti vasi altera mensa,
E ricca di vivande elette, e care.
Era qui ciò, ch'ogni stagion dispensa,
Ciò che dona la terra o manda il mare,
Ciò che l'arte condisce: e cento belle
Servivano al convito accorte ancelle. (G.L. x. lxiv)
[Where the shadows were thickest, by the sound of the clear waters, she made them prepare on the grass a sumptuous

table, decked with sculpted vessels and laden with choice, expensive meats. On it was the produce of every season, whatever the earth brings forth or the sea yields, whatever the culinary art can flavour: and a hundred, attentive hand-maids served at this feast.]

There are many other possible parallels. The haunted wood which leads to the Castle has much in common with the haunted wood in which the heroes of the *Gerusalemme* meet their particular temptation. The pastoral retreat in the realm of Indolence at points echoes the rural retreat enjoyed by Erminia. After all, Thomson had read Tasso as well as Spenser and was not positively trying to imitate either. His poem, therefore, is at once strikingly independent of both of its predecessors, yet at points reminiscent of either the one or the other. In this connection, it is important not to allow the obvious debt to Spenser to obliterate the lesser but nonetheless important one to Tasso. In addition, the fact that both Thomson and Tasso were, on their own admission, attracted emotionally to the very sensuous indolence they were intent on condemning, produces in their poems a more complex psychomachia than in the *Faerie Queene*, a strong sense of loving where one must reject. Other minor arguments could be adduced to account for a perceived closeness between the *Gerusalemme* and the *Castle*. For example, the latter's scope is much more specific than either of its two models. But the problem of indolence, the thematic centre of Thomson's poem, is highlighted more obviously by Tasso, being the particular weakness of his major hero, Rinaldo. Spenser, as MacKillop admits, allows the problems of the Bower of Blisse to merge into the greater pattern, having 'other knights and innumerable other scenes and episodes to convey various aspects of his doctrine'.

There is very little by way of direct borrowing in *The Castle of Indolence* but echoes and parallels do abound. Thomson's acknowledged debt, not only to Tasso but also to Dante, is a genuine one and as he also relates the central theme to his earlier experiences in Italy and to the effect exerted on him by Italian landscape painters, it becomes clear that the specifically Italian influence on this poem is not only extensive but extremely varied.

¶ A detailed study of the Italian line in Byron's verse would require a book on its own. A prolific writer, he spent almost eight years in Italy after leaving England and wrote extensively during his stay. His knowledge of Italian, his interest in Italian politics and his involvement with the 'Carbonari' are all well documented.

I shall confine myself to studying three works, each showing a different type of Italian influence, hoping that those readers who wish to look further will turn to one of the many full-scale analyses of his work.

The finest of his direct translations is the *Morgante Maggiore of Pulci*, so fine indeed that one wishes he had completed the project and not confined himself to Book 1. He retells the tale of Gan's treachery and jealousy of Orlando, the latter's angry departure from Charlemagne's court and defeat of the two giants, Alabastro and Passamonte. The third and fiercest giant Morgante is converted to Christianity and returns with Orlando to the abbey which earlier he had been terrorising. The book ends with the discovery of a cuirass for Morgante and the ill-assorted pair set off together in search of further adventures.

Pulci's epic with its mixture of religious seriousness, satire and pure burlesque appealed to Byron, whose own *Beppo* is in the same tradition, although immediately influenced by Whistlecraft. Moreover, he found it much easier to recreate the 'ottava rima' than he did Dante's 'terza rima' in 'Francesca of Rimini'. But before we turn to an examination of the skill with which the translation was effected, let us look briefly at the motivations behind that translation as expressed in the Advertisement. First he did so to improve his Italian, acknowledging the particular problems involved in gaining complete mastery of a tongue, which initially seems easy. Secondly (in Renaissance fashion) he is anxious to acquaint English speakers with a work of value hitherto unknown to them. But there is also a historical motivation. The talents of Pulci and Boiardo, according to Byron, played a large part in forming the *Orlando Furioso* of Ariosto, while Pulci also influenced Berni and Whistlecraft. Byron presents the poem, therefore, as an enjoyable work in its own right and as the precursor of even greater compositions.

It is true, as some critics have argued, that in some instances Byron's translation is an improvement on the original. He creates atmospheres with a surer touch than Pulci, as in Stanza 11:

Ma la Fortuna attenta sta nascosta,
Per guastar sempre ciascun nostro effetto . . .
[But watchful Fortune stands hidden, always ready to thwart our every plan.]
But watchful Fortune, lurking, takes good heed
Ever some bar 'gainst our intents to bring.

The use of the evocative 'lurking' in line one and the introduction of the visual image in line two intensifies the effect of foreboding more plainly presented by Pulci. Often Byron uses the final couplet strongly to clinch the preceding argument. In Stanza 23 the Abbot has described their constant vigil against the giants, ending forcefully:

> But now, if here we'd stay, we needs must guard
> Against domestic beasts with watch and ward.

Alliterative effects are also skilfully contrived to highlight humorous incidents. Thus in the Italian, when Morgante fires his arrow at a pig, we are told that it 'appunto ne l'orecchio lo 'ncarnava' [pierced its flesh exactly in the ear], while in Byron's version, it '*p*ierced a *p*ig *p*recisely in the ear'. At other times it is used to emphasise more serious matters, such as the awesomeness of the heroes, even in death:

> And pagan Passamont died unredeem'd,
> Yet harsh and haughty . . .

It is in small details like these that Byron's translating art resides and in the *Morgante Maggiore* he came across a work which so appealed to his temperament that, one senses, he found the normally tedious job of converting one language into another (very dissimilar in sound and structure) a labour of love.

Marino Falieri (like *The Two Foscari*) is not a translation, nor even a close adaptation of an Italian drama. Thematically it can best be seen as a political play, which makes several important points about freedom and particularly the value of intellectual freedom, which despite their generality do prove consistent with the aims of the 'Carbonari'. The poet was himself very much concerned at the Austrian control of Venice and it is easy to see that a plot in which the Doge allied with the people against a corrupt oligarchy would appeal to him. Yet undeniably he made more specific criticisms and allied himself more unequivocally with the 'Carbonari' in other works, notably *The Prophecy of Dante.* I am not, therefore, primarily concerned with its relevance to Italian politics but with the fact that it is written in a mode very close to that regularly adopted by one of Byron's literary heroes, the tragedian Alfieri.

In advancing this argument, I am aware both of the fact that Otway's *Venice Preserved* has claims to be regarded as an analogue and that some earlier critics have overstated the closeness between *Marino Falieri* and Alfieri's *La Congiura de'Pazzi*, seeking to turn inevitable and general parallels based on similar plots and plot structures into evidence of particular borrowings. Yet the case that Byron was, in *Marino Falieri*, writing with an eye on Alfieri's practice has the strongest possible backing, Byron's own. In a letter to Moore he admits, 'My object has been to dramatise like the Greeks . . . striking passages of history, as they did of history and mythology. You will find this very unlike Shakespeare; and so much the better in one sense, for I look upon him to be the worst of models, though the most extraordinary of writers. It has been my object to be as simple and severe as Alfieri, and I have broken down the poetry as nearly as I could to common language.'

Anyone reading *Marino Falieri* and a tragedy by Alfieri together, as Byron advised Moore to do, will be struck by obvious similarities. The Unities are carefully observed (even to the extent of perverting that 'history' which both claimed to revere); historical topics are nonetheless chosen and historic truth adhered to for the most part; there is action but the majority of it is cerebral – long monologues couched in quite simple diction but expressing the noblest of thoughts; there are no passages of comic relief and the authors share a number of rhetorical tricks including the piling up of rhetorical questions and exclamations, the use of successive brief, elliptical sentences and a love of lists. Byron is thus siding with the 'classical' line in drama, as had the only major Scottish playwright of the seventeenth century, Sir William Alexander. But among the many dramatists who followed a similar course he has chosen Alfieri as his particular model.

That said, I see no difficulty in supporting those who believe that *La Congiura de'Pazzi* lies behind *Marino Falieri*. In Byron's play, the ancient Doge reluctantly agrees to join a conspiracy to overthrow the ruling oligarchy. His joining is crucial and once it is gained the plan is put into action with the signal being the tolling of bells. The conspirators are defeated and die offstage. In *La Congiura* old Guglielmo reluctantly agrees to join the conspiracy run by his son Raimondo to overthrow the ruling Medicis. His joining is crucial and once it is gained the plan is put into action, the tolling of bells again being the signal. The conspirators are defeated and die offstage. Inevitably there are differences. Marino Falieri dominates Byron's play, but Raimondo is a more powerful figure than the vacillating Guglielmo in Alfieri. The voice of feminine counsel is in Byron, that of old Marino's wife, in *La Congiura* young Raimondo's. But knowing Byron's acquaintance with Alfieri's writings, he must have been aware that he was to some degree following a pattern earlier established in that play. The modes are similar. Byron's awareness of Alfieri's status as guide and mentor is unchallengable. It is only when one goes beyond this reasonable position and tries to establish particular echoes or to argue that a woman helping her husband in each play is a feature unique to Byron and Alfieri rather than a

commonplace in 'revolution' tragedies that the comparison becomes forced and unconvincing.

Finally, there are a number of poems in which Byron uses his
knowledge of Italy and its people to put across his own philosophical, political or literary ideas. These include 'The Lament
of Tasso', the 'Ode on Venice' and *The Prophecy of Dante* but
perhaps most interestingly Book 4 of *Childe Harold's Pilgrimage.*
There, as the pilgrim eventually reaches the end of his journey he
does make some direct comments concerning the great men of
Italian literature concluding powerfully that this land, now without its own freedom, was and is the guardian of art and religion:

> Yet, Italy! through every other land
> Thy wrongs should ring, and shall from side to side;
> Mother of Arts! as once of arms; thy hand
> Was then our guardian, and is still our guide;
> Parent of our Religion! whom the wide
> Nations have knelt to for the keys of heaven!
> Europe, repentant of her parricide,
> Shall yet redeem thee, and all backward driven,
> Roll the barbarian tide, and sue to be forgiven.

This open admiration for Italy and her traditions is an important
line in the fourth book. It is after all in Italy that the poet/pilgrim
solves some of his earlier problems and transcends others. The
waters of Venice which open the passus lead via the Thrasimene
lake, the Cascata del Marmore and various rivers to the concluding image of the ocean. He comes via these images of flux and
conflict to a vision calm and unchanging. In the same way his
experiences in Italy have eventually brought him to a knowledge
of that eternal source of all life and energy, which the ocean
symbolises.

If this is true in terms of the broader pattern of the book, it is
equally true that the various cities are used in part to develop
themes which have been with us since the pilgrimage began and
in part to explain the pilgrim/poet's reaction to them. The
opening Venice sequence, for example, once more begins the
opposition between Art and Nature. On one level it is Nature
which does not die – for as the 'palaces', signs of man's temporal
triumphs, crumble, beauty remains. The poet states explicitly:

> . . . but beauty still is here.
> States fall, arts fade – but Nature doth not die.

On another level, however, true art is proved immortal. Tasso
may be dead and the great era of Italian creative art passed, but it
remains in the minds of those who appreciate it. Likewise the
glories of Venice cannot themselves die so long as there are

artists who have celebrated them. So natural beauty is proved superior to the 'arts' of conquest but true art has an immortality which defeats the natural processes of time. Venice's example becomes the centrepiece for the most thorough analysis of an argument, which has haunted the pilgrim from early on in his voyage.

Venice is also used as a poignant example of the values of liberty and the ways in which they can give way to humiliation and tyranny but these ideas reach their true crescendo in Rome. Contemplation of the glories of past Empire contrasted with today's ruins and subjection leads him to a pessimistic conclusion:

> There is the moral of all human tales;
> 'Tis but the same rehearsal of the past,
> First freedom, and then Glory – when that fails,
> Wealth, vice, corruption – barbarism at last.
> And History, with all her volumes vast,
> Hath but one page, – 't is better written here
> Where gorgeous Tyranny hath thus amass'd
> All treasures, all delights, that eye or ear,
> Heart, soul could seek, tongue ask . . .

These conclusions do not represent a final truth. The pilgrim is always perceiving parts of the truth, accepting then qualifying them. But, like Piers Plowman, his geographical pilgrimage in appearance is really a pilgrimage of the mind. Venice, Rome, Florence *exist* but primarily they teach lessons about art, liberty and exile.

Each statue, building, ruin has its contribution to make towards this learning process and although there is no clear movement towards a divine revelation, there is at least the sense that he is beginning to understand the nature of self and pilgrimage. In particular the setpiece at St Peter's coming at a period of despair does point to the possibility of transcendental values which man, by definition, can only understand in part and piecemeal:

> Our outward sense
> Is but of gradual grasp – and as it is
> That what we have of feeling most intense
> Outstrips our faint expression; even so this
> Outshining and o'erwhelming edifice
> Fools our fond gaze, and greatest of the great
> Defies at first our Nature's littleness,
> Till, growing with its growth, we thus dilate
> Our spirits to the size of that they contemplate.

By the time we leave the pilgrim at the end of Book IV, the specifically Italian background has disappeared and he is still far from knowing all. But he has made the gigantic step of understanding the limitations of human knowledge, achieving this both in and through Italy.

¶ James Thomson, author of *The City of Dreadful Night*, was, like his namesake, influenced by Italian writers – most notably Dante and Leopardi. His interest in the works of the latter had begun by 1867 when he translated *Copernicus* for the *National Reformer*. Within a year he had published twelve translations and by the beginning of 1870 he had completed about 100 pages of an essay on the poet. For this he had read the 650 letters of the *Epistolario*, translating many of them. The reasons for his interest are not far to seek. Thomson was, like Leopardi, a melancholiac and found in the Italian's pessimistic philosophy confirmation of many of his own views.

In the 1860s and 1870s Thomson begins to include quotations from Leopardi in his works. For example, the opening chapter of his haunting prose phantasy, *A Lady of Sorrow*, describes the poet's first meeting with the lady and how his intense love merges with a desire for death. This is, of course, the very theme of Leopardi's 'Amore e Morte' and so, fittingly, Thomson concludes the chapter by citing the opening four lines of that poem:

Fratelli, a un tempo stesso, Amore e Morte
Ingenerò la sorte.
Cose quaggiù sì belle
Altre il mondo non ha, non han le stelle.
[Brothers, fate engendered Love and Death at the same moment. There is nothing else so beautiful down here on earth nor up amid the stars.]

Similarly the celebrations of nature and the laments on lost innocence contained in 'The Naked Goddess' and 'Proem' remind one strongly of Canto VII, 'Alla Primavera'. And in each case Thomson reassures us that the parallel is real, not imagined. 'The Naked Goddess' has as its epigraph the following lines from 'Alla Primavera':

Arcane danze
D'immortal piede i ruinosi gioghi
Scossero e l'ardue selve (ogge romito
Nido de' venti).
[Mysterious dances of immortal feet shook the steep mountains and the thick woods (today they are but the remote nest of the winds).]

while the phrase 'O antique fables', which opens both the first and last stanzas of 'Proem', derives from the continued title of 'Alla Primavera', 'O delle favole antiche'.

Yet, Thomson's fame rests squarely on *The City of Dreadful Night*, the poem in which he confronts the hell of his own pessimism. Again we are given a clear hint that both Dante and Leopardi may have influenced the work, for the three epigraphs are taken respectively from Canto III of *Inferno*, from Leopardi's Canto XXIII, 'Canto notturno di un pastore errante dell'Asia' and from the same poet's 'Coro di Morti'. Professor Schaefer in his book on Thomson argues that by the time of composing *The City*, the poet's interest in Leopardi was on the wane and that Dante's voice is more frequently heard. My own research would support that view. Certainly there are occasional brief echoes from the *Canti* but the major links with Leopardi are general and thematic. That is to say, in *The City* we find re-stated the Italian poet's vision of the world as a desert traversed by a despairing pilgrim, overcome by 'noia' and seeing only in death an escape. Both accept as rational the option of suicide. Thomson's Preacher teaches his congregation of shades that if life cannot be borne it is only proper to end it as soon as possible. Both stress Nature's indifference to man's fate and both come finally to strong anti-Christian conclusions (Thomson in *The City* xiv, xvi and xx; Leopardi most obviously in 'Ad Arimane').

Yet in a sense this is no more and no less than what we would have expected, given our knowledge of their shared creeds. By contrast, the Dante echoes are, almost without exception, used to highlight the greater hellishness of Thomson's hell. Perhaps the most obvious example of this technique is to be found in the sixth section. There, as in the *Inferno*, there is a door and above it the same inscription:

I reached the portal common spirits fear,
And read the words above it, dark yet clear,
'Leave hope behind, all ye who enter here.'
(cf. Dante: Lasciate ogni speranza, voi ch'entrate.)

But Thomson at once raises the additional question, that some have no hope to leave and so are not even able to enter Hell:

So I returned. Our destiny is fell;
For in this Limbo we must ever dwell,
Shut out alike from Heaven and Earth and Hell.

Likewise Dante had two guides initially, both well intentioned and admired by him. Virgil was his prime authority on earthly life and Beatrice his spiritual mentor. Together they guided him for his greater understanding through scenes from which he stood apart. In *The City*, Thomson is only too involved and, instead of Virgil, has the shadowy guide of Section ii, uncertain where he is going himself and pointing out the shrines of the theological virtues. In Section xviii he is led by Blake, his own early poetic hero, but one whose vision of a return to youthful purity is now mercilessly satirised. Instead of Beatrice, the embodiment of life after death, Thomson has his dead fiancée Matilda first of all carrying her heart in her hand as a lantern, symbolising the failed potential of their relationship, and later in her bier worshipped by the poet who sees no life after death.

Through such variations on Dante, Thomson drives home to his readers the deeper pessimism of a vision in which

> There is no God; no Fiend with names divine
> Made us and tortures us; if we must pine,
> It is to satiate no Being's gall.

To one who thinks in this way both the allegoric method and the three-tiered structure of *La Divina Commedia* may be poetically impressive but it remains philosophically ridiculous. As Dante soars eventually to the *Paradiso*, Thomson remains confined within his earthly City, imprisoned by his temperament and beliefs. By frequently echoing phrases and situations from the Italian poem, he drives home to us this contrast in its starkest possible form.

¶ I have intentionally kept my analysis of the novel separate from the discussion of poetry and drama for, of course, the situation with regard to the later genre is very different. To begin with, while Italy had led the way in poetry and drama, providing much outstanding material to imitate, the Italian novel developed much slower than, and in different ways from its British equivalent. There was, for example, very little Italian interest in the picaresque novel, while in the first half of the nineteenth century there was so little activity, that Pacifici can remark, 'Aside from Manzoni's great novel *I Promessi Sposi*, no other work of imaginative prose was written in that period'. It is therefore not surprising to find detailed imitation working from Scotland to Italy rather than the other way round. Walter Scott inspires Manzoni and Grossi; the stronger tradition guides the weaker one.

On the other hand, from the early Romance experiments of Urquhart, through Smollet to Scott we do find Italian places, characters and even books playing a minor but significant part in the early Scottish novel. Sir Thomas Urquhart is a seventeenth-century writer and his work *The Jewel* with its strong autobiographic element and complex form could only in the loosest possible sense be termed a novel but it does have links with Scott in particular.

For example, Urquhart like Scott preferred to romanticise figures drawn from the past, and like Scott he enjoyed painting in the European background of the Grand Tour. In the central story of *The Jewel*, the two fuse. The Scottish hero, Crichton, based on an actual nobleman, proves his various skills at foreign courts, notably Paris and Mantua. When depicting these events Urquhart is careful to draw on his own first-hand observation of Italian customs, thus giving to his Romance the air of reality. When Crichton amuses the Mantuan court with his miming and play-acting, the overall force of the scene derives largely from this authentic Italian context:

> Nevertheless it happening on a Shrove-Tuesday at night, at which time it is in Italy very customary for men of great sobriety, modesty, and civil behaviour all the rest of the year, to give themselves over on that day of carnavale, as they call it, to all manner of riot, drunkenness, and incontinency, which that they may do with the least imputation they can to their credit, they go maskt and mum'd with vizards on their faces, and in the disguise of a Zanni or Pantaloon to ventilate their fopperies . . .

The suggestion of the 'commedia dell'arte' tradition leads neatly into the virtuoso performance in the histrionic arts given by Crichton himself. Even this is narrowed down for Urquhart informs us that Crichton's dramatic accomplishments were based on the very stylised form of that art, practised at Venice. Thus, 'he begun to prank it, à la Venetiana, with . . . a flourish of mimick and ethopoetick gestures'.

Not only does Italy provide a background for the major events in the story of Crichton. Inevitably, various Italian noblemen enter the tale in their own right. Frequently, these characters are presented in terms of a trait then generally held by foreigners to be characteristically Italian. It was, for example, supposed that Italians were the finest European swordsmen and Scott later makes much of this. Thus the 'admirable Crichtoun' must prove Scots superiority by defeating one of that nationality on the field of combat. But note how Urquhart specifically relates his opponent's particular excellence to the national reputation of his countrymen:

> A certain Italian gentleman, of a mighty, able, strong, nimble, and vigorous body, by nature fierce, cruell, warlike, and audacious, and in the gladiatory art so superlatively expert and dextrous, that all the most skilful teachers of Escrime,

and fencing-masters of Italy, which in matter of choice professors in that faculty, needed never as yet to yeild to any nation in the world, were by him beaten to their good behaviour, and by blows and thrusts given in, which they could not avoid, enforced to acknowledge him their over comer . . .

This incident is based on a factual meeting but the movement from connecting a character's ability with national reputation to creating fictitious figures embodying national traits is a small one. Both types abound in the early Scottish novel and are anticipated here.

Italian influence on Urquhart takes the form of geographic setting, characterisation and various details of culture and customs. As such it plays quite an important part in establishing credible surroundings for romantic events, in bringing variety to the 'dramatis personae' and in explaining variances between Scottish and Italian behaviour. The lack of closer imitation is a matter of choice, for Urquhart, like his hero Crichton was a master of many European languages, including Italian. Indeed, the great sixteenth/seventeenth-century cult of imitation properly reaches its zenith with his magnificent 'translation' of Rabelais. In *The Jewel* he decides to express his European interests in another way and his method was to be adapted by Smollett and Scott. Certainly he read and appreciated the great Italian authors. When Crichton dies, it is noted that some of the elegies 'were composed in so neat Italian, and so purely fancied, as if Ariosto, Dante, Petrarch, and Bembo had been purposely resuscitated'. But their works contribute nothing more than this to *The Jewel*, which as surely stands at the start of one tradition in the use of foreign influence as his version of Rabelais stands at the end of another.

¶ Tobias Smollett's links with Italy belong to the later period of his life. In 1764 and 1765 he visited the country in the course of a tour, which he later recorded in *Travels through France and Italy*. His longer stay (1768–71) covered the last years of his life and his tomb is to be found on the banks of the Arno between Leghorn and Pisa. Further, the evidence would suggest that he either began his study of Italian just before starting his tour or improved upon a very scanty knowledge gained before that date. As his picaresque novels *Roderick Random, Peregrine Pickle* and *Ferdinand Count Fathom,* as well as *Sir Lancelot Greaves* were all completed before this crucial journey, it is not surprising that Italian influence on them is slight. As increased knowledge of

Italy and Italian coincided with two novels *Humphry Clinker* and *The Adventures of an Atom,* whose focus is firmly on British life and politics, the *Travels* must remain the most interesting topic for the comparative critic.

Yet the sort of general influence detected in *The Jewel* is to be found in the novels. Even Roderick Random on one occasion finds Italian literature helping him to advance the course of his wooing. When Narcissa and her aunt are discussing 'a knotty passage of Tasso's Jerusalem', his advice is asked. They are astonished to find that Roderick, posing as a servant, knows the language. He therefore has to account for his knowledge in terms of his supposedly humble upbringing, 'I told her I had picked up a smattering of Italian during a voyage up the Straits'. The slight use of Italian in the novel is usually, as here, connected with social divisions. It helps to distinguish the upper classes, who may hold conversations in French or Italian, from the lower. It is also a distinguishing mark of the man of letters, as represented by Malopyn, but that is all.

The hypocrisy of this Italian veneer is more thoroughly satirised in *Peregrine Pickle,* which also sees the introduction of Italian characters. These, as in Urquhart, prove to be mere types founded on popular British preconceptions. One is a physician, educated at Pisa, but held by the stolid British characters to be a charlatan. The other is a fiddler who disguises himself as a count and in that guise abducts both the wife and property of the faithful servant Hadgi. Such stereotypes presumably delighted an audience already convinced of Italian duplicity, amorousness and medical incompetence.

In *Fathom* two major advances are made. The technique of using characters of different nationalities to provide variety and interest is more thoroughly developed. Spaniards, French and Italians mingle, allowing Fathom to demonstrate his skill as a linguist and a manipulator of simpletons. Also the tendency to present characters in terms of simplified national characteristics is here analysed by a character in the novel. Ratchkali, the treacherous Tyrolese adventurer, perceptively notes that when Englishmen quarrel with strangers they invariably have an opprobrious formula for them, such as 'a chattering Frenchman', 'a German hog' or 'an Italian ape'. More importantly, the anti-hero Fathom is set against the idealised chivalric figure of Renaldo, who, as his name suggests, has links with the *Orlando Furioso.* As the secondary focus of interest and as the lover who seems doomed to eternal disappointment, the parallel with Rinaldo is apposite. Yet his near madness and the eventual success of his quest bring him more clearly into line with Orlando and that is how he signs himself in his love letters to Monimia. As the true 'mirror of modern chivalry' in the novel and as the impassioned lover, Renaldo recreates the basic tensions of Ariosto's heroes. The hints are not extensive but they are clear.

Momentary influences from the *Orlando Furioso* can also be found in *Lancelot Greaves*. Although the basic idea of anachronistic knight-errant with comic squire is strongly reminiscent of *Don Quixote*, Smollett avoids excesses of farce and treats especially his hero's love for Aurelia Darnel on a level of higher seriousness. On this level Greaves is the true lover, driven into madness through being spurned by his lady. In this part of the study details from the *Orlando* are used, some of which suggest that Smollett had a knowledge of the original text as well as translations. Thus when, in Chapter 15, hero and heroine meet, we are told that,

> Aurelia shone with all the fabled graces of nymph or goddess; and to Sir Lancelot might be applied what the divine poet Ariosto says of the Prince Zerbino:
>
> Natura il fece e poi ruppe la stampa.
>
> 'When Nature stamp'd him, she the dye destroy'd.'

Greaves as character and novel suffers from the uncertain shifting of vision from 'Quixote' to 'Orlando' but Smollett is nonetheless consciously using European texts when moulding his story.

Humphry Clinker is deservedly his most famous novel and was written in Italy. Yet, because the focus is mainly on Britain, Italian references are for the most part of the general sort noted in *Random* or *Pickle*. But there is one marked difference. This lies in the number of parallels between Italian and Scottish society in the later book. It is an interesting comment on the focus of this novel, that all these comparisons are aimed at explaining the virtues or failings of *Scottish* life. Thus Bramble reminisces on the Lago di Garda and Albano but only to impress on Dr Lewis the beauty of Loch Lomond. In similar fashion, English travellers explain to English correspondents the state of Scottish peasants, sanitation and food by comparing them to their French or Italian equivalents. This is a new and unexpected twist on the idea of the 'universal family' of Europe. To the English, Scottish society is more of a mystery than Italian. In unreservedly embracing the European 'family' the English have ignored the closest relation of all!

The *Travels through France and Italy* is an epistolary work of considerable interest to those concerned with eighteenth-century Scottish reactions to Italy. Unfortunately Smollett's reaction, like Thomson's in *Liberty*, is largely one of disillusionment. The major centres of his attention are Genoa, Pisa, Florence and Rome, each affording him new grounds for discontent. Like Thomson he is aghast at the extensive poverty, permeating all levels of society. In Genoa he highlights the plight of the poor noblemen who 'live with great parsimony in their families, and wear nothing but black in public'. Characteristically he supports this with an anecdote, telling of one such who sent his son to buy a frugal meal. On discovering that the boy had spent a zecchino, the old man burst into tears and cried out, 'Ah figliuolo indegno! Siamo in Rovina! Siamo in precipizio!' [Ah wretched son! We are ruined! We are on the edge of the abyss!].

Smollett's jaundiced view of both France and Italy (earning him from Sterne the nickname 'learned Smelfungus') was probably partly due to his bad health. Certainly the sad picture he draws of Pisa in the *Travels* differs markedly from the quite enthusiastic account given in the letters written from there during his second stay. Illness may also account for his obsession with the poor accommodation at inns. His vein of dry humour directed against such places reaches its climax when they put up at a small village inn near Arezzo:

> The house was dismal and dirty beyond all description; the bedclothes filthy enough to turn the stomach of a muleteer; and the victuals cooked in such manner that even a Hottentot could not have beheld them without loathing.

Other travellers were shocked at conditions in European inns but few expressed their reaction with Smollett's acidity.

If such outbursts are not likely to endear Smollett to Italians, they do contribute to the dramatic interest of the work, which, as Louis Martz has shown, is not merely a haphazard collection of letters but bears signs of artistic organisation. In particular the Italian journey and the comments on Nice are separated from the actual time sequence and dealt with in an 'artificial series of letters', showing little sign of being part of a personal correspondence, though many of the others clearly are.

This discovery shows Smollett to have had some experience of organising an epistolary work prior to *Humphry Clinker*. It also removes the *Travels* from the context of the unplanned, spontaneous record to that of a hybrid between such a record and a controlled work of art. Particularly, it would now appear that the Italian comments are largely the considered judgment of Smollett on that country, rather than casual reactions to places on passing through. Martz has also proved that some of the long judgments on architecture and art are in fact translated from works Smollett had been reading. Long portions of the account of Rome, for example, are based on a guide book entitled *Roma Antica, e Moderna* (Rome, 1750), while most of the comments on the Uffizi Gallery in Florence stem from Giuseppe Bianchi's *Ragguaglio Delle Antichità e Rarità che si Conservano Nella Galleria Medicea-Imperiale di Firenze* (Florence, 1759). What therefore appear to be personal comments for the benefit of friends are culled from his reading and intended for a wider audience.

Evidence of this sort allows us to regard the Italian portion of the *Travels* as a considered work of art, having close relations with the epistolary novel and showing particular imitation from Italian texts, as well as the more general influences implied by the very nature of the journey. This book and to a lesser degree the novels show Smollett using Italian material in a way which was to anticipate Scott. But unlike the latter he has never been very popular with the Italian reading public. Perhaps this is because of his somewhat negative view of country and people, perhaps because of his interest in the picaresque mode so largely ignored in Italy, perhaps because of his distinctively Scottish sense of humour. But whatever the reasons, his lack of popularity seems to me a pity for he is a craftsman of great skill and originality.

¶ In direct contrast, Walter Scott became Europe's most popular novelist. Yet his use of foreign material is rather similar to Smollett's. Like the earlier novelist he visited Italy towards the end of his life, noting down his comments in journal form. But this was 1832, the year of his death. It produced only the draft of the short story *El Bizarro*, a rather melodramatic tale of the 'banditti', which makes the most perfunctory use of its Italian setting. It is not here in age that we should look for Scott's Italian enthusiasms but in youth. At college he had alienated the Greek department by upholding Ariosto's superiority to Homer in a class essay. And although Hoole's translation was his first introduction to both Tasso and Ariosto, he soon began to read these authors in the original as well as Dante, Boiardo, Pulci and others. Later he will attribute his success as a novelist to early reading of Boiardo and Ariosto (once a year) and *Don Quixote*.

Like Hume, Adam Smith and Carlyle he wrote critically on Italian literature in the *Essays on Chivalry, Romance and Drama*. This is an appreciation of European writing, with Italy one contributor among many. Again, however, the name of Ariosto looms large. He places him in the context of old Romances, showing the greater control over the form of his poetry, when compared with later practitioners. One gathers pleasure, he tells us, from 'the extreme ingenuity with which Ariosto gathers up the broken ends of his narrative, and finally weaves them all handsomely together in the same piece'. Scott's own novels with their apparently limitless flexibility, yet overall authorial control; their tantalising mixture of realism and romance present a variation on Ariosto's model as here defined.

In linking the *form* of Ariosto's Romance with Scott's novels, I am not indulging in an arbitrary critical fancy. Scott himself accepted it and his narrators often force home the point. In Chapter XVI of *The Heart of Midlothian*, Scott prefaces a discussion of Robertson and Effie with the comment:

> Like the digressive poet Ariosto, I find myself under the necessity of connecting the branches of my story by taking up the adventures of another of the characters, and bringing them down to the point at which we have left Jeanie Deans. It is not, perhaps, the most artificial way of telling a story, but it has the advantage of resuming what a knitter . . . might call our 'dropped stitches'.

Scott here not only models himself on Ariosto; the narrator's modest tone contrasts with the overt praise given to his technique in the *Essays*. The use of digression, the changing of scene, the tying up of loose ends, had there been related to the traditions of Romance and the author's greater ingenuity. This may not prevent a critic's distaste for, say, the last few chapters of *The Antiquary*, where an eldest son, an explanation about treasure and startling new information about the hero are all needed to bring the plot harmoniously to a close, but it does place such a method in its proper context and clarifies the author's own attitude to it.

This formal similarity to the Romances of Ariosto means that Italians could readily accept Scott's novels, unlike Smollett's use of the Picaresque. But the influence of Boiardo, Tasso and Ariosto also extends to *content*. This does not imply re-creation of scenes earlier encountered in the *Orlando Furioso* or *Gerusalemme Liberata*. At the simplest level, it involves frequent retreats to the periods immortalised in these works. The martial opposition between pagan and Christian is at the centre of both *Gerusalemme* and *Orlando Furioso*. The Crusades are the centre of *The Talisman* and *Count Robert of Paris*, while playing a part in *Ivanhoe*, *Anne of Geierstein* and others. Specific debts are usually in the form of parallels. In *The Talisman*, the hermit of Engaddi is twice explicitly compared to Tasso's Peter the Hermit on whom he is modelled. In *Count Robert of Paris* Prince Tancred's beauty is described in the following terms: 'Remarkable for that personal beauty which Tasso has preferred to any of the Crusaders, except Rinaldo d'Este, the creature of his own poetical imagination.' It will be noted that in this instance, the Italian parallel is used not only to boost Scott's character but to distinguish him from the fictitious characters of Romance. Thus Italian Romance is employed sometimes to determine the form, the topic and the characters of Scott's novels but also to point by way of contrast, the reality of his own heroes.

A variation on this is to present a character who has been brought up on Romances and then bring him face to face with actuality. Scott's knowledge of Italian literature thus becomes part of his skill in *characterisation* and *theme presentation*. The most obvious example is Waverley. Having read numerous romantic poems from Pulci onwards, his expectations are initially Romantic. He expects Donald Bean Lean to be 'a stern, gigantic ferocious figure, such as Salvator would have chosen to be the central object of a group of banditti'. The contrast between imagination and fact is shattering and at length Waverley sheds the excesses of his Romantic fancies. What is less frequently realised is that the reader is also conditioned into sharing Waverley's initial romantic vision, and thus into sharing his disillusionment. The narrator plays a large part in this. He tells a story, whose form has much in common with the Italian Romance; he compares his aims to Tasso's: 'I may be here reminded of the necessity of rendering instruction agreeable to youth, and of Tasso's infusion of honey into the medicine prepared for a small child.' Often too his outlook merges with that of his hero, as when he describes a scene, which 'was not quite equal to the gardens of Alcina; yet wanted not the "due donzellette garrule" of that enchanted paradise', or compares Flora to 'a fair enchantress of Boiardo or Ariosto'. Through the form of the novel we undergo the very temptations of Romance to which Waverley has succumbed and Scott's success at this level relies on his own wide acquaintance with his hero's reading matter! Even the characters who scorn Romances are not entirely ignorant of Italian writers. Fergus MacIvor of all people can quote these lines from the first canto of Folengo's *Orlandino*; although he has chosen his passage well:

Io d'Elicona niente

Mi curo, in fé di Dio, ché 'l bere d'acque

(Bea chi ber ne vuol) sempre mi spiacque!

[I care nothing for Helicon, I swear to God, for drinking water (let he who wishes do so) was ever a torment for me!]

And the fact that he considers their author a 'crack-brained Italian Romancer' cannot obliterate the fact that he has read and retained them in their original form.

More Romance reading goes into this, the first of Scott's novels, than any other. But even here, if the world of Romance is seen as largely one of illusion, then like M. Jourdain's world of the 'mamamouchi', it is also a world in which the sane must participate in order to accommodate the major protagonist. Re- actions vary from Fergus's scorn to Rose's admiration via the sly irony of Flora, 'he can admire the moon and quote a stanza from Tasso'. But, in the opening *Waverley* novel, every major character has to define himself in relation to the values of Romance, thus permitting Scott to make the widest possible use of his personal reading in Italian literature.

If the works of Ariosto and Tasso play a large part in advancing one of the principal themes in *Waverley*, they play a different part in advancing the *plot* of *Rob Roy*. Francis Osbaldistone wants to translate the *Orlando Furioso* and Scott even provides us with an example of his efforts. This ambition, however, is skilfully worked into his romantic relationship with Die Vernon. Pretend- ing a similar literary passion she at once works along with and shamelessly flatters him ('Now that the passage in Dante is made so clear!'). Later, when he realises her cunning, his ex- pression of outrage is itself dictated by his ruling passion: 'The society of half a dozen of clowns to play at whisk and swabbers would give her more pleasure than if Ariosto himself were to awaken from the dead.' Smollett in *Roderick Random* had used one instance of this sort. Scott develops on this example until Francis's copy of Ariosto almost becomes a character in the novel.

All the novels discussed so far have been appropriate recep- tacles for Scott's references to Italian literature. They do occur, however, in less promising places. In *Old Mortality* we find Gib- bie's pike being compared to 'the celebrated thrust of Orlando which, according to the Italian epic poet, broached as many Moors as a Frenchman spits frogs'. And in *The Monastery*, we can scarcely be astonished to hear the Sub-Prior back up an argu- ment by citing these lines from Ariosto:

O gran bontà dei cavalieri antiqui!
Erano nemici, eran' di fede diversa.

[O the great goodness of the knights of old! They were adversaries, they were of different beliefs.]

In short, Italian literature becomes part of the texture of Scott's novels. In some it supplies only a chance quotation or parallel, in others it may play an essential rôle in determining form, content, themes or characters. But in very few indeed is it non-existent.

Other cultural activities make their presence felt too. The high quality of Italian music is referred to in *A Legend of Montrose*. A Spagnoletto decorates the home of Oldbuck. The heroes of *The Abbot* in their 'gay Milan armour' mix with other figures brandishing 'Andrea Ferraras' or 'poniards of Parma'. Piercie Shafton steps it out in his 'peach-coloured doublet of Genoa velvet' while the pros and cons of the 'Commedia dell'arte' are considered in *St Ronan's Well, Redgauntlet, The Abbot* et al. Yet if Scott's wide knowledge of such things undoubtedly lends background authenticity to his works, it is still an 'external' knowledge culled from books. His knowledge is extensive but it is received and, for example, rather many of the Waverley heroes possess 'Andrea Ferraras'!

Nonetheless Scott may fairly be said to surpass Smollett in building up an authentic Italian background for his novels. He also continues, though not so enthusiastically nor so acidly, Smollett's satirical vein. Dr Lundin in *The Abbot* clearly belongs to the same family as Squire Burdock's son in *Humphry Clinker*. At once a fop and a pretender to extensive knowledge, he persists in sprinkling his language with quotations in Latin and Italian, thus rendering himself universally unintelligible. Here again we have an Italian 'type' conforming to British prejudices – as in Urquhart and Smollett. For the most part Scott's Italian characters are of this sort. The charlatan Dr Baptista Damiotti in *My Aunt Margaret's Mirror* is the natural successor to the Paduan doctor in *Peregrine Pickle*. Inevitably too there are a group of Macchiavellians (as popularly interpreted). Montserrat in *The Talisman* is by all accounts cunning and self-centred enough but he must give way to the Campo Basso of *Quentin Durward* and *Anne of Geierstein*. A supposed supporter of Charles in the latter novel, he 'waits but the highest price to sell his Highness like a sheep for the shambles'. In the end he does exactly this and is memorably summed up by Arthur Philipson: 'a more accomplished traitor never drew breath, nor one who drew his net with such success.' This element of treachery is also regularly attached to Italian characters in Scott. Why, we even find Henry Warden in *The Abbot* using it as a formulaic epithet of the sort scorned by Ratchkali in *Ferdinand Count Fathom*. Montserrat's conspiracy against Richard in *The Talisman* brands him a traitor. Even Galeotti in *Quentin Durward*, based though he is on a historical character fits into this last classification and is presented as a type.

These repetitions, whether they be of 'Andrea Ferraras' or Macchiavellian traitors, show that Scott's advance on the example of Smollett is not as great as might at first appear. His wider reading and antiquarian interest enable him to produce a wider range of detail but such details are drawn from a limited pool of interests and recur from novel to novel. Foreign characters, too, seldom escape from 'nationality typing', though Scott is a bit more subtle than Smollett. Nonetheless they are both predominantly looking at Italy from the outside, through literature rather than experience. At the same time, Italian culture and characters do add colour to the novels. The repetitions are only noticeable when the Italian material is drawn together in an exercise like this. It is unlikely to spoil enjoyment of a particular work. Also, it must be argued that the humourised creation has as much literary validity as any other. As such, Damiotti and the others may be deemed successful. Yet the limitations on Scott's knowledge of Italy made such characters the bounds of its expression. More individualised portraits would have proved difficult indeed.

These reservations are important, but the major result of an enquiry such as this one is to highlight the crucial part played by Italian material in Scott's novels. It is particularly effectively integrated into *Kenilworth* and *Peveril of the Peak,* set in English courts where Italian culture dominated. To begin with, the limitations above noted become the limitations of the characters themselves, like Scott viewing Italy from outside. In *Kenilworth* the literary line is dominated by Elizabeth's interest in her godson Harington's translation of Ariosto. Yet she also uses Boiardo's *Orlando Innamorato* to provide the image of a fairy using a sword-blade as a mirror and can cite Italian proverbs. Other arts play their part, including the 'great basins of Italian marble' in the gardens at Kenilworth. All these references are worked unobtrusively into the novel and so establish the historical authenticity of a court imbued with the vigour of the Italian Renaissance.

It is this development of a greater variety of Italian influence which places Scott at the head of the new type of imitation begun in the late seventeenth and eighteenth centuries. Now Italian social life can become part of a Scottish novel. While earlier ages had concentrated on conscious, literary imitation, the European culture of the eighteenth century encouraged also these social, political and geographical influences which the artist could introduce less selfconsciously. We have seen the poets and the dramatists adapting to this re-definition to some degree and in sharply different ways. With the novel, it is true to say that Urquhart, Smollett and Scott are working within the same broad tradition. Of the three, however, it is Scott whose literary and cultural researches, skill in character depiction and genuine interest in the cosmopolitan philosophy of his predecessors enable him to realise more fully what the others achieved only in part. His novels are distinctly Scottish but they aim at relating Scotland to a clearly perceived European base – one of the major reasons for their extreme success abroad. The two ingredients, Scottish and European, are essential elements in Scott's popularity and although the former is more obvious, to regard him as a European novelist is a less distorting generalisation than to focus on passages of Scots dialect and label him parochial. Properly viewed he and Byron are the finest examples of Scots writers benefiting from Italian life and letters in the eighteenth and nineteenth centuries. Drummond might have been surprised to see some of the forces against which they had to battle in that period and interested at the broader definition of 'imitation' which began to emerge then. But he would have been proud to accept both as his natural successors.

IV

The Second Renaissance

It is not difficult to understand in retrospect why the literatures and especially the poetry of Scotland and Italy have resumed the harmonious interrelationship earlier enjoyed in the reign of James VI. If we look at the situation first of all from the Italian perspective we see that the loss of political unity resulted in increased cultural isolation, a position only partly modified by re-unification at the end of the nineteenth century. At the beginning of the twentieth century the 'Crepuscolari' and 'Futurismo' movements began the transition away from this unhealthy situation but only by the end of the Second World War was the Italian voice once more confidently heard within a European context. Then, writers of the status of Saba, Ungaretti, Montale and Quasimodo guaranteed that this voice would not only be heard but heard with respect.

The Scottish situation proves in many ways similar. From the nineteenth-century tendency towards parochialism and that lack of confidence which betrays itself by overconcern with the past, we move into a surer national consciousness with the First World War. And then there comes MacDiarmid's powerful cry for a literature which will be at once Scottish and European. Mac-Diarmid himself tended to look elsewhere than Italy for inspiration but others – notably Morgan, Garioch, Henderson, George Campbell Hay and Douglas Young – found in the energetic new Italian movement as well as earlier Italian writing similarities in thought and technique which they were to use with profit in their own verse.

¶ It must therefore be clear from the outset that in focusing on four poets only, I am choosing from a much larger possible number and in so doing at once reflecting the variety of the wider movement and expressing my own critical preferences. In beginning with Edwin Morgan I turn to a polymath whose translations and adaptations range from Russian to Old English. He has paid homage to the Italian writers of the past (Petrarch, Ariosto, Tasso, Michelangelo) in *50 Renascence Love Poems* and his contributions to Lind's *Lyric Poetry of the Italian Renaissance*. He has successfully used Scots as a medium in his adaptations of Tuscan Folk Songs. But his most impressive work is in English and reflects his admiration for particular members of the new Italian movement, as well as (arguably) their spiritual leader Leopardi.

Moving from James Thomson (called the 'English (sic) Leopardi') to Morgan does provide us with a bridge from one century to another but on every level Morgan's understanding of the poet proves more subtle and more profound. His sensitive translation of 'La Ginestra' ('The Broom') expertly recreates Leopardi's picture of the broom flourishing again on the desolate sides of Vesuvius and then becoming a symbol for the poet's own grim courage in facing a future without illusions. He and the broom will be destroyed but neither will have succumbed to the temptation of praising a malevolent fate as if it were a caring God :

> E piegherai
> Sotto il fascio mortal non renitente
> Il tuo capo innocente :
> Ma non piegato insino allora indarno
> Codardamente supplicando innanzi
> Al futuro oppressor.

[And you will bend without a struggle your innocent head under the deadly burden. But it will not be a head bent down in vain until that time, in cowardly pleading before your future oppressor.]

MORGAN

> And you will bend
> your innocent head with unreluctant nod
> under that deadly load :
> but not a head you bent till then in vain
> with cowardly entreaty praying for
> your future killer's grace.

The same care is shown when he provides his English version of 'Il Sabato del Villaggio' ('Village Saturday') a work whose title, concern with the poverty of the agricultural worker and even some of its character vignettes, is reminiscent of Burns's 'The Cotter's Saturday Night'.

> E intanto riede alla sua parca mensa,
> Fischiando, il zappatore,
> E seco pensa al dì del suo riposo.

[And meanwhile the labourer with his hoe goes home, whistling, to his frugal meal, and thinks to himself about his day of rest.]

MORGAN

> while the farm worker with his hoe returns,
> whistling, to his meagre meal,
> and thinks how his one day of rest comes round.

Of course Leopardi's vision lacks the strong line of Christian consolation present in Burns's poem as well as the sense of everything having its rightful place in a carefully ordered scheme. Time for Burns is benevolent; for Leopardi it highlights cruelly the contrasts between youthful hope and aged frustration, urging us at best to grab briefly moments of happiness however delusory.

One should not be misled by the closeness of the translations quoted above into thinking that Morgan always follows his originals passively. It is first of all no easy matter to move from a language which pronounces double consonants and has no silent or clipped vowels into one in which the opposite is the case. Like Drummond, Morgan is always alive to the needs of rhythm, choosing his words with precision. Also, and again like Drummond, close comparisons almost always show him making those deft changes of emphasis and meaning which separate the true translator from the mere mimic. An analysis of the relation between 'To Himself' and Leopardi's 'A Se Stesso' should make this clear.

> Or poserai per sempre,
> Stanco mio cor. Perì l'inganno estremo,
> Ch'eterno io mi credei. Perì. Ben sento,
> 4 In noi di cari inganni,
> Non che la speme, il desiderio è spento.
> Posa per sempre. Assai
> Palpitasti. Non val cosa nessuna
> 8 I moti tuoi, né di sospiri è degna
> La terra. Amaro e noia
> La vita, altro mai nulla; e fango è il mondo.
> T'acqueta omai. Dispera
> 12 L'ultima volta. Al gener nostro il fato
> Non donò che il morire. Omai disprezza
> Te, la natura, il brutto
> Poter che, ascoso, a comun danno impera,
> 16 E l'infinita vanità del tutto.

[Now you will rest for ever my tired heart. The last deception has perished, which I thought was eternal. It has perished. I clearly feel that in us not just the hope of sweet illusions, but the wish for them too has been extinguished. Rest for ever, heart. You have throbbed enough. Nothing merits your beating, nor is the earth worthy of your sighs. Life is bitterness and tedium; never anything else; and the world is mud. Calm yourself now. Despair for the last time. To human kind fate's only gift was death. Now despise yourself, Nature, the evil power which, hidden, works for the communal ill, and the infinite vanity of everything.]

MORGAN

Now, and for ever, you may rest,
My worn-out heart. Dead is that last deception.
I had thought love would be enduring. It is dead.
4   I know that my hoping, and even
My wishing to be so dearly deceived, have fled.
Rest, and for ever. The strife
has throbbed through you, has throbbed. Nothing is worth
8   one tremor or one beat; the very earth
deserves no sigh. Life
has shrunk to dregs and rancour; the world is unclean.
Calm, calm. For this
12   is the despair. What gift has fate brought man
but dying? Now, undo in your disdain
nature and the ugly force
that furtively shapes human ills, and the whole
16   infinite futility of the universe.

In the opening lines Morgan maintains both the repetitive emphasis of (Perì – dead) and the alliteration (cor; ch'eterno; credei – dead; deception; dead) but in different ways and with different effects. Also, by introducing the word 'love' in line 3 he makes explicit the nature of the deceit before Leopardi does. If he loses something of the immediacy of the self-address in lines 7 and 8 by omitting an equivalent for 'tuoi', he has earlier transmitted the sound and continuity of the heart's throbbing more effectively than Leopardi's brief 'Assai/Palpitasti'. Wisely too, he freely translates lines 9 and 10 and chooses to render the urgency and sound patterns of 'T'acqueta omai' as 'Calm, calm'. Indeed throughout there is clear evidence of the poetic craftsman sensitively re-working his original, striving for closeness but always alive to those occasions when different techniques and emphases are called for.

Earlier I used the example of Drummond to explain the nature of Morgan's translations. And if Drummond, for all the breadth of his borrowings, clearly had a favourite poet in Marino, so Morgan has a favourite in Montale. Now the difficulties of providing English versions of this poet's subtly suggestive works cannot be over-emphasised. To reconvey a unique world in which the objects observed have a value in themselves but often also a strong personal association and an impersonal symbolism is the sort of task which would seem most obviously to have attractions for an enthusiastic masochist. Morgan, however, is fully aware of the problems and of that genius which has made Montale so highly regarded internationally. Part of Morgan's reason for translating so much of his verse is, I suspect, the original Renaissance one, that here is a poet of such greatness that his message and methods MUST be made available to a wider public and if the translator will, by the nature of his calling, fall short of perfection, then so be it – the attempt has been made.

As critic, Morgan defines the 'world' of Montale as 'a distinctive place, sometimes beautiful, sometimes frightening and desolate. We move into it gradually as the imagery of sense-impressions from poem to poem builds up a strongly felt atmosphere which in the end can be seen to pervade the whole verse: a shimmer, a play of light on water and on crumbling walls, a whiff of camphor, a fact glancing in a mirror.' Now, while there are times when I feel his unfeigned admiration for the Italian poet along with the translation problems earlier outlined lead him into that very timidity or passivity which is hardly ever evident in his versions of Leopardi, it is equally true that often he comes closer than anyone else to recapturing the lights and shades of Montale's ever-shifting, ever-suggestive universe.

Particularly effective is his rendering of 'Spesso il Male', that tantalisingly dense lyric where both life's evils and its boring sameness are conveyed through daring imagery. Morgan's skill lies in maintaining, at times even strengthening these images, while also sustaining the original work's onomatopoetic force and starkness of diction.

> Spesso il male di vivere ho incontrato:
> era il rivo strozzato che gorgoglia,
> era l'incartocciarsi della foglia
> riarsa, era il cavallo stramazzato.
> Bene non seppi, fuori del prodigio
> che schiude la divina Indifferenza:
> era la statua nella sonnolenza
> del meriggio, e la nuvola, e il falco alto levato.

> [I have often met the anguish of life; it was the choked stream which gurgles, it was the crumpling of the dried up leaf, it was the horse prostrate on the ground. I knew no good, apart from the miracle which divine Indifference reveals: it was the statue in the torpor of midday, and the cloud, and the falcon high in the sky.]

> Often I've met the wrong of the world in my walk:
> there by the strangled brook with its guttural song,
> there with the puckerings of the thirsty tongue
> of a parched leaf, there by the horse that fell and shook.
> Little I knew but what I saw in a rune,
> a vision of the divine Unconcern:

there by the statue in the drowsy sun
at noon, and the cloud, and the heaven-climbing hawk.

Equally impressive are his versions of the 'Sarcofaghi', poems in which Montale looks at sculptured sarcophaguses, describes in detail the carvings, and emphasises the vast gulfs between life, life through art and death. Or there is 'Arsenio', a work which has much in common with Leopardi's 'A Se Stesso', being an imagined conversation with oneself aimed at discovering the ultimate purpose of life. Characteristically, Montale refuses to share the pessimism of his predecessor as the conclusion, in Morgan's version, indicates:

or if one
word can become your friend, this is perhaps
a sign, in one spontaneous hour, Arsenio,
of a struggling life ascending now through yours
and wind-borne with the ashes of the stars.

My own favourite is his translation of the famous 'La casa dei doganieri' ('The Customs-Officers' House'). Here Morgan re-conveys in all its complexity the poet's reaction on seeing once again a landscape and a house which used to hold a special meaning for him and his loved one. Now she thinks of it no more ('You don't recall the house of the customs-men'). He knows their relationship is dying ('a thread is still unwinding') but desperately strives to maintain some contact ('I hold an end of it yet'). This theme of a place at once linking past with present and emphasising the painful difference of lost union reminds one of Hardy, but not even at his best did the English poet present it as hauntingly as does Montale. It is to Morgan's immense credit that even here, in a poem as technically skilful as it is emotionally disturbing, so little is lost in the movement from one language to another.

¶ Unlike Morgan, Robert Garioch does not translate from a wide variety of Italian writers, preferring to concentrate on one; nor is his chosen model a leading modern poet, but the nineteenth-century 'sonnet machine' Giuseppe Belli. Unlike Morgan, whose dominant tone in his Italian translations is grave, searching, philosophic, Garioch has at once the comic ebullience and the satiric wit of Rabelais. Also, having fought in Italy, he has a number of first-hand war poems and a book of memoirs, *Two Men and a Blanket*, to add to his translations. Above all, while Morgan chose to write predominantly in English, Garioch composes in Scots, with an ease that might make some later 'makars', struggling for an adequate vocabulary, blush with shame.

Before we discuss those brilliant adaptations from Belli, it is
necessary not only to look at the war poems but also briefly at the
way in which incongruous invoking of grand Italian visions of the
past may be used in his original verse to give a new slant to
Scottish life and thought. In 'The Muir' for example, we begin
with 'Great Dante's Hell' but only to underline that Scotland is
not to be outdone in its own brand of hellish experiences:

> In Glesca and in Hell muckle is kent
> of reik and flames, by deevils and by men
> levan or hauf-gaits levan, and they ken
> in Edinbrugh the wey to freeze the ghaist
> in ice as thick as thon in Dante's den.

The witty association of Edinburgh with ice, Glasgow with flames
intensifies the joke, but even this pales into insignificance when
the Scot searches around for an equivalent of Paradise!

> and Paradise preclair wi seraphim,
> aureat in itsel, altho mair dim
> to Scottish ingyne (Dante's anaa, I dout)
> was human in a wey, wi aa that's grim
> in yirdlie dispensations seindit out –
> Badenoch in simmer, wi nae clegs about.

Here, of course, the hilarious anti-climactic effect is tinged with
the more serious implication that for the average Scot the grandi-
ose visions of Hell and Heaven have simply no relevance.

As a war poet Garioch is neither prolific nor overtly emotional.
Even in the midst of conflict and pain he maintains that wit and
clear-sighted satiric vision which characterises most of his verse.
Listen to his account of counter-commands in the first stanza of
'Hysteria':

> Left! Richt! Left turn! Richt turn! Richt about turn!
> I birl, thinking nae mair nor I maun,
> for this is meant to reive me of wits;
> they need me as a mummer, no' a man.

Even in the touching 'Letter from Italy', in which he gains com-
fort from thinking that he and his beloved, though far apart, may
both see the Pleiades, there are moments of wit and cool self-
analysis. Surrounded by crawling enemies, he finds the 'large red
bugs' more ingenious and more frightening. Raising his eyes to
the stars and making them a bond of love, he cannot resist
pointing out in a parenthesis that, in happier days, such contemplation had bored him stiff.

Perhaps his finest poem about the war describes a bout of mal-
aria he suffered near Benevento. Looking down from the heights,
his senses confused, the camouflage paint takes on a new life:

> It is a broun desert, wi lizards that hae baith
> a cleidin of licht-green scales, and kinna dark-green feet.
> It is a mottie jungle pentit full of faces
> of men wi broun faces, green hair and dark green lips,
> wroucht in ae pattern, and moniefauld, and seen
> maist clear. . . .

As this clarity is lost and the poet relapses into unconsciousness,
the poem too tails off into incoherence:

> cannae be ours, green in the,
> broun in the,
> the.

These poems with their careful artistic and emotional control;
their refusal to sink into self pity and their ability to convey horror
in the very act of understating it, seem to me superior to the
breastbeatings of Brooke and Owen.

But without doubt Garioch's greatest debt to Italy comes from
Belli. The Italian poet came across della Porta's Milanese poems
and decided that he would do the same for Rome. Bible tales,
religious creeds, religious hypocrisy, amusements, festivals and
character studies all attract his attention, building up a variegated
and exciting picture of the city. Garioch was attracted to him first
of all because here was another poet writing in a dialect and doing so both humorously and satirically. Also Belli's chosen mode
was the sonnet, a form that Garioch found especially challenging.

Belli wrote no fewer than 2279 sonnets, leaving Garioch quite
a range to choose from! In the following analysis I shall concentrate on the topics which seem most to have appealed to the
Scottish poet and the way in which he transformed his material.
To begin with, many of Belli's works ironically diminish religious
seriousness. Pomposity is deflated; sermon styles are parodied
and even central tenets of faith viewed in a mocking, non-
spiritual vein. As an example of this last type we may take no.273
'Er Giorno der Giudizzio'. In the opening quatrain the atmosphere of the barracks square is carefully evoked and the angels
made to sound more like foul-mouthed sergeants than God's
spiritual servants:

> Cuattro angioloni co le tromme in bocca
> Se metteranno uno pe ccantone
> A ssonà: poi co ttanto de voscione
> Cominceranno a ddí: 'Ffora a cchi ttocca.'

> [Four huge angels with trumpets in their mouths will place
> themselves, one in each corner, to blow them: then with
> enormous voice they will begin to say: 'Out those who are
> called'.]

This for Garioch becomes:

> Fowre muckle angels wi their trumpets, stalkin
> Til the fowre airts, sall aipen the inspection;
> They'll gie a blaw, and bawl, ilk to his section,
> In their huge voices: 'Come, aa yese, be wauken'.

The translation is reasonably close in one sense but undeniably the Roman judgment has been turned into a Scots one. The last command would have done that on its own! It is also noteworthy that both the size and the earthiness expressed by 'angioloni' and 'voscione' are maintained by 'muckle' and 'huge'. Garioch, like Urquhart, learned quickly that the way to transmit an already exuberant voice is to match or go beyond it. And although this is a trifling example, it is a technique used regularly and with great success throughout his sequence.

But the major reason for the Italian-Scottish transition lies in the precise use of language. Garioch has the knack of putting into the mouths of his characters the very word which takes us straight into Cowcaddens or the coffeehouses of Morningside. Nowhere is this gift put to greater effect than in the series of character vignettes. There is for example Belli's 'avocato Cola' whose pride forbade him to ask for charity, so slowly he ate up all his goods and died alone. He becomes for Garioch, Maister Mac-Coll ws, whose fate inevitably is the same:

> syne, at the end, in thon chair, wi nae breid,
> nae water, nae bit fire intill the grate,
> steekit his een and, in stairvation dee'd.

An even more precise placing in time and space comes with 'The Mowdert Spinster' where Garioch quite explicitly removes Belli's 'La Zitella Ammuffita' from nineteenth-century Rome to twentieth-century Edinburgh. As both original and adaptation are among the finest sonnets in their authors' respective sequences, they merit quoting in their entirety:

> È inutile pe mmé, ssora Nunziata,
> De dimannamme si mme faccio sposa.
> Io nun zò Llutucarda, io nun zò Rrosa,
> Per èsse bbenvorzúta e ariscercata.
> Pe mmé ppovera mmerda è un'antra cosa.
> Nun me sò inzin' adesso maritata,
> E ccreperò accusí; perch'io sò nnata
> Sott'a cquella stellaccia pidocchiosa.
> Ciarlàveno der coco; ma ssu cquello
> Nun c'è vverzo da facce capitale:
> Sta ppiú fforte der maschio de Castello.
> Bbasta, aspettamo un po' sto carnovale,

Si ccapitassi quarche scartarello:
Lassàmo fà ar Ziggnore e a ssan Pasquale.
[It's useless as far as I'm concerned, Nunziata, to ask me if
I will marry. I am not Lutegarda, I am not Rosa, who are
made to be loved and sought after. For me poor scum it's a
different matter. I have not married until now and I will die
in the same state; because I was born under that mangy
malign star, Virgo. There was talk about the cook; but there
is no chance of being able to count on him: he is more
adamant than the angel on Castel Santangelo. Enough, let's
wait for this carnival in case some reject might come along:
leave it to the Lord and San Pasquale.]

GARIOCH

It's nae guid speiran at me, Maistress Cant,
to let ye ken hou suin I'm gaun to mairry.
Ah'm no like Rosie, and Ah'm no like Sairey,
juist made fir luve, thit onie chiel wad want.
Bit as fir me, puir dirt, it's different.
No mairriet yet, some hope! I wait and weary
and blame my sterns; whit a weird I cairry:
Virgo, the stingiest in the firmament.
There wes some kinna clash about the cook;
nae chance wi him, ye canna bank on thon:
he staunds mair firm nor the Castle Rock.
Aweill, bide till the Festival is on,
in case it brings some orra bit of trock:
leave it to Gode and St. Pasqual' Baylon.

There is first the movement in time and space. By referring
specifically to the 'Festival' and comparing the cook's firmness to
the 'Castle Rock', Garioch faces us with a specifically twentieth-
century Edinburgh spinster. But that is on one level only. By
entering wholly into the mind and thoughts of Belli's creation he
also confirms that the type of the self-pitying, frustrated spinster
lives in every age. A large part of his skill lies in finding the exact
Scots idiom or colloquialism to match the Italian one. Thus
Llutucarda and Rrosa's doubtful morality is expressed through
the two verbs 'bbenvorzúta' and 'ariscercata', but Rosie and
Sairey are slyly condemned in phrases more akin to Scottish
gossip than any exact translation. They are 'juist made fir luve,
thit onie chiel wad want'. There exactly is the spite and the envy.
Indeed of the two narrators, it is Garioch's who has the harsher
tongue, the stronger line in expletives. Belli's stops short of the
indignant expostulation – 'No mairriet yet, some hope!' and if
her cynicism/despair finds its focus in the 'scartarello' of line 13,

she is again outdone in vividness and contemptuousness by the
Scots woman's 'some orra bit of trock'. It is arguable that the
harsher vowel sounds and the more clipped consonants of Scots
fits it better than Italian for this type of bitter diatribe. Certainly
Garioch makes sure that alliteration is called to the spinster's aid
whenever necessary – ('There was some kinna clash about the
cook,') – and generally achieves a harshness of sound not present
in the more lyrical original.

Garioch and Morgan, therefore, may be very different poets
with very different literary preferences but they share not only a
deep love of Italian literature but that rare gift of being able to
adapt Italian originals into English or Scots with imaginative flair
and linguistic precision.

¶ Of the younger generation of poets, interested in translation
and adaptation, Robin Fulton stands out as the one with the
greatest potential. Like Morgan he writes mostly in English and
has a wide range of languages including Italian. Like Morgan
too, he is particularly interested in the modern movement, having
produced in 1966 *An Italian Quartet,* which contained versions of
work by Saba, Ungaretti, Montale and Quasimodo.

These poems were composed when Fulton was beginning his
career and they are certainly not without flaws but they do show
that attention to rhythm and careful choice of word and image
which were to become a feature of his later work. In the brief
introduction he defines them as lying 'somewhere between translations and imitation'. They will have succeeded he believes if
each can 'stand on its own feet as English verse yet fulfil the same
kind of intentions as the original fulfils'. My own impression is
that usually they are quite close translations, but most do achieve
an identity of their own and only a few do weaken the original
poetic message.

If, for example, we look at his version of Saba's 'Primavera', we
will find Fulton keeping remarkably close to the Italian:

> Primavera che a me non paci, io voglio
> dire di te che di una strada l'angolo
> svoltando, il tuo presagio mi feriva
> come una lama. L'ombra ancor sottile
> di nudi rami sulla terra ancora
> nuda mi turba, quasi anch'io potessi
> dovessi
> rinascere. La tomba
> sembra insicura al tuo appressarsi, antica
> primavera, che piú d'ogni stagione

crudelmente risusciti ed uccidi.

[Spring who holds no joys for me, I want to say of you that, turning the corner of a street, your promise struck me like a blade. The still slim shadow of bare branches on the still bare earth disturbs me, as if I too could, should, be reborn. The tomb seems uncertain at your approach, ancient spring, which more than any other season cruelly brings back to life and kills.]

FULTON

Spring, in whom I find no pleasure,
I want to tell you that facing you
suddenly round a street corner
hurts. The shadow, still intricate,
of bare branches on the still bare earth
unsettles me, as if I too
am expected to return to the beginning.
Not even the grave seems secure
against your persuasions, you, spring.
with your age and your unwilting youth,
your harsh renewal, your murdering.

The problem is, that although Fulton seldom deviates from the original, whenever he does he seems to lessen that sense of horror felt by age and grief when suddenly nature demands it be young and gay. 'Hurts', for example, is much weaker than the image of the blade wounding, while the menace of 'il tuo presagio' is entirely lost, and it is surely not the 'return to the beginning' which is at the base of the poet's horror, rather the call to spring up bright and fresh again. Structurally too, there is no attempt to find an equivalent for the rhyming strengthening which leaves 'dovessi' isolated in line 7.

Fulton expressed the fear in his introduction that some might feel he had turned good Italian poems into bad English ones. In fact this happens very seldom but I do feel that 'Spring' must be numbered among the small group of failures. Equally, there are occasions when a competent translation or adaptation is weakened by the failure to find a means of conveying formal qualities which obviously had been of importance to the Italian writer. Inevitably Ungaretti with his attempts to maintain control through typographical arrangements poses the major problem here. Fulton provides two versions of 'Veglia', both in their own way impressive but neither having an equivalent for the single word backbone of – 'massacrato', 'digrignata', 'penetrata'. The challenge is, I know, a difficult one but it seems merely to have been sidestepped.

Yet there are many excellent adaptations in this collection and if I take both my examples from the section devoted to Quasi-modo, that is because I feel the Scottish poet to be most at home with that author, even when coping with the strange language and obscure metaphors of *Acque e terre*. You will, for example, go a long way before you come across a more sensitive treatment of 'Antico inverno':

> Ancient winter: desire for your bright hands
> burning between the flame and the flame's shadow,
> smelling of oak, roses, death.
> Words are like finches stubbing for grain
> and suddenly snowed out.
> A dab of sunlight, a halo, then mist;
> and the trees and ourselves made of the morning air.

But perhaps the finest work in the whole collection comes from a later collection *Giorno dopo giorno*. The complex mixture of emotions roused by 'Dalla rocca di Bergamo Alta' as the poet in a mood of intensified sensation hears at once the cries of birds, sees the beauty of the moon, and feels for himself a brief moment of unreal peace among the horror, is not easy to recreate. But Fulton, using rhetorical tricks such as alliteration and verbal repetition does succeed in drawing us inexorably to that climax of sad yet threatened peace:

> The February moon made her way
> full-face, but to you a shell
> of memory, ablaze in its silence.
> Now, you are walking in your own quiet
> among the cypresses: here the rage
> relaxes in the green of dead boys
> and in the distance the pity looks like joy.

Fulton was (and hopefully will continue) to produce technically more satisfying collections of European adaptations, but despite some minor weaknesses, *An Italian Quartet* has much to commend it both in and for itself and as an introduction to the writings of the foremost modern Italian poets.

¶ Hamish Henderson, like Garioch, saw war in Italy and has a number of poems re-creating that time of tension and despair. But while it is Garioch's clearsightedness and wry wit which first impress the reader of his verse, one is most affected by Henderson's tenderness and compassion not only for his fellow soldiers but for all humanity. This aspect of his talent is perhaps best expressed in 'Fort Capuzzo', where he describes one of the allies pausing to ponder beside a German grave:

> For there will come a day
> When the Lord will say – Close Order!
> One evening, breaking a jeep journey at Capuzzo,
> I noticed a soldier as he entered the cemetery
> And stood looking at the grave of a fallen enemy.
> Then I understood the meaning of the hard word 'pietas'
> (a word unfamiliar to the newsreel commentator
> as well as to the pimp, the informer and the traitor).
> His thought was like this. Here's another 'Good Jerry'.
> Poor mucker. Just eighteen. Must be hard up for manpower
> or else he volunteered, silly bastard. That's the fatal
> *the – fatal* – mistake. Never volunteer for nothing.
> I wonder how he died? Just as well it was him though
> and not one of our chaps – Yes, the only good Jerry
> as they say, is your sort, chum. Cheerio, you poor bastard.
> Don't be late on parade when the Lord calls 'Close Order'.
> Keep waiting for the angels. Keep listening for reveille.

The thoughts follow each other naturally, in no clearly ordered sequence. The diction, simple and colloquial, is absolutely in keeping with the presumed 'persona', while there is an interesting conflict between what the man has been taught to feel about his enemy ('the only good Jerry as they say') and what he actually does feel in his greater generosity. In this case the poem's simplicity is its strength.

Henderson's Italian translations and adaptations are often drawn from the slightly lesser known modern poets. One of his most recent is a brilliant rendering of Dino Campana's 'Chimera'. I shall, however, concentrate on a group which were in a sense forced on him. He chose to translate Ruggero Orlando's influential essay 'On Contemporary Italian Poetry'. As Orlando quoted freely from all the poets he chose to highlight, Henderson naturally had to follow him. Thus, beside versions of poems by Montale, Ungaretti and other front runners, we find works by, for example, Francesco Monterosso and Giorgio Bassani. Their concern with the futility of war is expressed simply and unaffectedly almost as if they were consciously following Gramsci's appeal for a less erudite type of art. As this straightforward, humane sort of writing comes very close to Henderson's own, it is not surprising that it also produces some of his best translations. Vividly Monterosso captures the horror of fighting the Germans in his own country once the underground has become revolution:

Fucile e baionetta l'ho gettato
Sputando sangue e fiele ad una svolta,
Al mio paese sono ritornato
Per riabbracciare i cani di una volta.

Scarc! Dalla finestra dirimpetto
Qualcuno ha sventagliato la mitraglia,
Un ragazzo col capo dentro il petto
Sanguina in mezzo al fango ed alla paglia.

[I have thrown away my gun and bayonet, spitting blood and bile at a turning, I have returned to my village to embrace once more the dogs that I once knew. Scarc! From the window opposite someone has sprayed a burst of machine gun fire; a boy with his head sunk into his chest is bleeding amidst the blood and the straw.]

Maintaining his directness, Henderson turns this into:

I've thrown away my rifle and bayonet,
Spitting blood and gall at the bend of a road.
I've come back now to my own village
to embrace the men they used to call 'dogs'.

Scarc! Some-one at the window opposite
has opened an arc of fire like a fan.
A boy with his head collapsed in his chest
is bleeding in the midst of mud and straw.

Equally effective and affecting is Bassani's lament of a partisan killed at Naples during the 'Four Days' insurrection:

Non piangere, compagno,
se m'hai trovato qui steso.
Vedi, non ho più peso
in me di sangue. Mi lagno
di quest'ombra che mi sale
dal ventre pallido al cuore,

Portami fuori, amico,
al sole che scalda la piazza
al vento celeste che spazza
il mio golfo infinito.

[Do not cry comrade if you have found me lying here dead. See, I have no more weight of blood in me. I lament this shadow which is moving up from my pale belly to my heart. Carry me outside, friend, into the sun which warms the square, into the azure wind which sweeps over my endless bay.]

Given the fact that he is writing within the confines of a critical essay and so trying to convey as accurately as possible the meaning of the various pieces, Henderson clearly cannot indulge in overly free adaptation. But his translation is as powerful as the original:

> Don't cry, comrade,
> if you've found me lying here.
> Look, there's no more weight
> of blood in me. I complain
> of this shadow spreading
> from my white stomach to my heart,
>
> Carry me outside, friend,
> to the sun heating the square
> to the heavenly wind sweeping
> my gulf of infinity.

Like Byron, Henderson became involved in the Italian political scene during his stay there and perhaps he will mainly be remembered within the Italian context, not for his original poetry, his adaptations or translations good as all these undoubtedly are, but for being the first to translate into English the 218 letters written by Antonio Gramsci, the leading Italian communist during his prison detention from 1926 till 1936.

Viewed from whatever angle – philosophical, political, literary or personal – these are documents of the first importance. Gramsci's great courage, his will to survive, come through early on when he maps out a four-point plan designed to keep his mind active throughout what he well knows may be a prolonged captivity. He intends a work on the Italian intellectuals of the last century according to 'the cultural currents of the time, their diverse modes of thought etc.'. Even more ambitiously he wants to embark on a study of comparative linguistics. And as if this was not enough, he wishes to study the plays of Pirandello and compose a long essay on the popular taste in literature. The most interesting letters are addressed to his sister-in-law Tania. It is to her he explains his views on the Jewish question, gently trying to overcome her remaining prejudices; it is to her he discusses the different social groupings in Milan and Rome, enthusiastically proclaims that he may have solved a crux in Dante or argues for the existence of two conflicting Italies one visible, one invisible. Yet other correspondents and personalities play their part – his wife Julia increasingly unable to shoulder the burden of separation and eventually suffering a severe nervous breakdown; the two sons Delio and Julik, separation from whom adds to the poignancy of Gramsci's situation, and his mother whose death in 1932 was for a long time concealed from him. Seldom have a group of letters so powerfully conveyed the strength and the miseries, the fears and the hopes of a man and a nation. Henderson's translation conveys all this and is certainly not his least important contribution to the cultural interrelationship between Scotland and Italy.

¶ If our strong modern poetic tradition has profited from its Italian counterpart, what can be said about Scottish drama? The usual cynical answer to this question is 'As little as possible, please'. But even the near moribund Scots theatre has since the 1950s showed signs that prophecies of its death were somewhat premature. Among the newer plays was one by an actor, the late Victor Carin. It was based on Goldoni's *Il Servitore di due Padroni*. As *The Servant o' Twa Maisters* it played to duly appreciative audiences but now appears to be forgotten even to the extent that I had to unearth one of the old Lyceum acting copies to pursue this study. Here, if ever, is a case for publication. Otherwise this racy, witty, very 'theatrical' farce is in grave danger of becoming only a memory cherished by those lucky enough to have seen one of the original performances.

Although Carin at times adapts freely and adds numerous conversations and pieces of stage business, he maintains the basic plot. As this is essentially slight, it need not detain us long. Truffaldino finds himself servant both to Beatrice (a girl disguised as a youth) and to Florindo, who loves her but has fled because he believes, erroneously, that he has killed her brother. The first comic focus then is on Truffaldino's efforts to keep each of his masters unaware of the existence of the other. As Beatrice is passing herself off as Federigo, her brother, however, another confusion arises. Federigo is promised in marriage to Clarice, who is in love with Silvio. Despite all Clarice's protestations, her aggressive father Pantalone demands that the earlier agreement be upheld. Farcical situation follows on farcical situation but inevitably all ends happily. Truffaldino confesses his ruse and marries the man-mad servant Smeraldina; Beatrice is re-united with Federigo, now safe in the knowledge that he is not a murderer and Clarice's betrothal to Silvio makes for the triple nuptials so often favoured in this kind of farce.

Carin's first alterations are of the most obvious kind. He writes in broad Scots and alters both names and locations. Federigo Rasponi of Turin thus becomes Andra Burnett o' Annamuck and Truffaldino Battocchio from Bergamo is transformed into

Archie Broon frae Dundee. The scene of the whole play moves from Venice to Embro and so on. But alongside these larger, and inevitable movements, there are numerous changes of detail, usually aimed at heightening some piece of witticism. In Act 1 Scene 2, for example, Pantalone and Silvio's father, Il Dottore Lombardi, are summing up Truffaldino, while he flirts with Smeraldina. In the Italian we read:

> Pant.: (piano al Dottore). Mi credo che el sia un
> sempio costù.
> Dott.: (piano a Pantalone). Mi par piuttosto un uomo
> burlevole.
> Truff.: (a Smeraldina) V.S. è la sposa?
> Smer.: Oh! (sospirando) Signor no.
> [Pant.: (quietly to the Doctor). I think this man is a fool.
> Dott.: (quietly to Pantalone). To me he seems more
> somebody to make fun of.
> Truff.: (to Smeraldina) Mademoiselle is the bride?
> Smer.: (sighing) Oh sir, no!]

The two exchanges are kept separate. Carin instead uses Archie's question wittily to divide the two old men:

> Alec (Dott.): (aside to Pittendree) The man's an idiot
> A'm thinkin.
> Archie (Truff.): (to Susie) Are ye promised yersel?
> Pittendree (Pant.): (to Alec) A'm thinkin he's sense
> eneuch.

Throughout the play, Carin is never afraid to make slight alterations like this – to change or re-assign speeches, omit or add passages, whenever he felt that farcical moments would thereby either be introduced or strengthened.

Apart from these alterations, there are three major areas in which Carin makes so strong an original contribution, that *The Servant o' Twa Maisters* can be seen to differ at times quite markedly from Goldoni's play. The first concerns characterisation, particularly the minor characters. He substitutes for the somewhat ineffective landlord Brighella, a loudmouthed landlady Mistress Gow, in whom he becomes so interested that she threatens in the first act particularly to distract attention from the principals. She is marked out first of all by her inability to say a thing once:

> Fairly that Sir, A said fairly that, an' honoured forbye,
> A said honoured.

Brighella had not suffered from this type of verbal repetitiveness. Nor was he blessed with Gow's knack of curt repartee:

> Gow: Weel, pit the saut cod i' the middle.

Archie: (Making a face) A canna thole saut cod.

Gow: Ye'll nae be eating it.

By making her a woman, Carin is also permitted to introduce some snide suggestions that she once had an affair with Pittandree; and when she recognises Beatrice's disguise her 'girlish' joy in the subterfuge ('O whit rare ploys, A said whit ploys') is more convincing and amusing than Brighella's slow and reluctant agreement to maintain the deception.

If this is the major character alteration, other changes in emphasis abound. Some are just part of Carin's more overtly farcical approach. Thus although Smeraldina is intent on catching any man, she is neither so desperate nor so devious as Susie and there is no equivalent in the Italian of Susie's contempt at her mistress's lessons in screaming to prevent molestation, when molestation is just what she wants! Others are due to the twentieth-century setting. Mary is much more aggressive when countering her father's wishes, while Clarice smoulders but is ever conscious of the duty owed by eighteenth-century daughters to their parents. And some are national. If the Scots women are every bit as outspoken and pert as their Italian equivalents, Carin wisely does not let his Scots men spout lyrical Latin rhetoric to their girls. In the last scene, for example, when Silvio is proclaiming his love to Clarice he bursts out passionately:

> Misurate dalla vostra pena la mia, signora Clarice, e tanto più assicuratevi che vi amo davvero, quanto più il timore di perdervi mi aveva reso furioso. Il cielo ci vuol felici, non vi rendete ingrata alle beneficenze del cielo. Coll' immagine della vendetta non funestate il più bel giorno di nostra vita.
>
> [Measure my suffering against your own, Signora Clarice, and be the more assured I love you truly, the more the fear of losing you had aroused my anger. Heaven wishes us to be happy, do not show yourself ungrateful towards the gifts of heaven. Do not darken the most beautiful day of our lives with the idea of revenge.]

When Sandy makes the same protestation, it is noticeable that the rhetoric is simpler, the higher flights of amorous fancy have been excised and the speech is half as long!

> Measure my agony wi' yer ain Mary, an' rest assured A love ye maist truly. Shairly ye'll no lat revenge spoil the maist beautiful day o' yer life?

Secondly, Carin was himself an actor and it is noticeable that the amount of stage 'business' is increased in his version. At the start of Act 1 Scene 13, Goldoni introduces a porter who is carrying Beatrice's case. This he gives to Truffaldino with the

minimum of trouble and without speaking a word. Carin introduces a comic mime and a hilarious dialogue, deriving its humour
from the fact that the porter is clearly half-witted. Episodes of
melodrama, real or affected, such as Archie's grief stricken lament at the death of the non-existent John, or Mary's studied
(but oh so brief!) faint when she learns Sarah is a man are also
additions, which add greatly to the zany humour of the Scots
version. The episodes concerning the setting of the table and the
serving of the guests, though present in the original are also
greatly extended, showing us that Carin is trying at once to
increase the overtly farcical elements in the drama and to give
fuller play to mime, action and visual effects generally.

The last important area to be studied is that of language.
Carin's Scots is pungent, snappy and heavily idiomatic. As a
result his work is much less sophisticated than Goldoni's but if
he loses some of the subtler moments of wit in the Italian original,
there are plenty of forceful Scots idioms and exclamations to
replace it. Here, for example, are Mary and Sandy indulging in a
somewhat vicious brand of flirtation.

> Mary: Sandy, Sandy, A love ye, adore ye, worship ye.
> O spick tae me Sandy.
> Sandy: Ye leein' trollop, gin ye love ony man it's Annamuck,
> an no me. A heard him tell ye tae mind yer oath.
> Mary: It's nae an oath tae *mairry*, Sandy.
> Sandy: Whit oath was it then?
> Mary: Dinna speir, Sandy, hae patience. A'm sworn tae
> silence.
> Sandy: That jist gaes tae proove yer guilt.
> Mary: Yer wrang Sandy, gin a *spoke* A'd be guilty.
> Sandy: An' wha swore ye tae silence?
> Mary: Andrew.
> Sandy: An' ye tell me there's naethin' atween ye?
> Away ye jaud, wi' yer lees.

Inevitably Archie is the leading exponent of the outraged exclam-
ation, as when he discovers he has mixed up the contents of his
masters' cases, and desperately confides to the audience, 'A've
pit the orra thing in the wrang pooch!' Or when he chides
himself with telling effect 'Weel Archie, mak a sauce o' this, an'
A'll hae naethin' mair tae dae wi' ye!'

The debts of Scottish drama to Italian are, as we have seen,
few. In choosing as he did, Carin set himself to imitate a writer of
great genius and subtlety but I am convinced that Goldoni would
have been much more appreciative of *The Servant o' Twa Maisters*

for all its alterations and innovations than the much more timid English translations, which are usually the non-Italian speaker's introduction to this fine play.

¶As far as the novel is concerned, there can be little doubt that the writings of Moravia, Pratolini and others have created new respect for Italian experiments in that genre but they have not directly influenced any of the five Scots novelists, whose work will be the focus of this last part of the book. Two of them, Norman Douglas and Compton Mackenzie, wrote before Moravia and all five are interested in Italy itself, its geography, its people or its politics rather than the compositions of particular authors. The two most important, Norman Douglas and Muriel Spark, settled in Italy, living there for many years. The others, Mackenzie, Eric Linklater and Allan Massie, were brought there by motivations as different as war and curiosity but each and every one was greatly affected by the country and used it as the setting for one or more novels.

Douglas is rightly best known for *South Wind* (1917) but before that his travel books *Old Calabria* and *Siren Land* had given ample evidence of his love for and understanding of Italy. They are complex works, frustrating for the reader who wishes a clearcut form and a simple message. And above all they are as much journeys into Douglas's own mind as into Southern Italy. This Douglas himself admitted, 'It seems to me that the reader of a good travel-book is entitled not only to an exterior voyage, to descriptions of scenery and so forth, but to an interior, a sentimental or temperamental voyage, which takes place side by side with the outer one; and that the ideal book of this kind offers us, indeed, a triple opportunity of exploration – abroad, into the author's brain, and into our own.'

Certainly those who come to *South Wind* via these books will be prepared for many things which may seem odd or even unsatisfying to others. To say the book is formless or without plot is unfair but like the travel books it is composed largely of short essays and disquisitions on a vast variety of topics. These are of course all topics dear to Douglas himself and although he cannot speak to us 'in propria persona', the views of the forthright Mr Keith, the philosophical Count Caloveglia and the erudite Mr Eames all come suspiciously close to ideas held by Douglas himself. As in the travel books, we dip into Italy's pagan past, consider its right to be once more the centre of an intellectual Renaissance, delve into the sources of Saints' Legends, discuss the influence of climate on character and do so in the company of vivid, often humourised characters.

From our particular point of view, the first thing to establish about *South Wind* is the existence of an extra character, the island of Nepenthe itself. It is in part an invention but as Ralph Lindeman stated, 'that it is more like Italy than like any place else is not surprising, since Douglas assuredly believed that the sunny south was the best hope of civilised men'. It is vividly realised for us in the very first chapter:

> Nepenthe became tangible – an authentic island. It gleamed with golden rocks and emerald patches of culture. A cluster of white houses where a playful sunbeam had struck a pathway through the vapours. The curtain was lifted. Half lifted; for the volcanic peaks and ravines overhead were still shrouded in pearly mystery.

This mixture of vivid clarity and shifting mists is of the utmost importance. It returns at the end when Count Caloveglia remarks on the Sirocco's passing:

> Sirocco is over for the present. The wind has shifted to the North. It brightens all nature. It makes one see things in their true perspective.

What both Nepenthe and the Sirocco offer is at once clarity and mist, a difficult and shifting truth, which in particular Northerners have difficulty in accepting. They find what they had considered absolutes – especially moral absolutes – are in fact contingent. They find it increasingly tempting to invert priorities and place, say, beauty above goodness; or to cast off the veneer of civilisation and partake of the pagan past. As Keith puts it:

> Northern minds seem to become fluid here, impressionable, unstable, unbalanced – what you please. There is something in the brightness of this spot which decomposes their old particles and arranges them into fresh and unexpected patterns. That is what people mean when they say they 'discover themselves' here.

The clearest example of this process in action is Bishop Heard. An Anglican bishop from Central Africa, he is the first character we meet, arriving at Nepenthe in the hope of visiting his cousin. Now, Heard has already learned in Africa the error of too rigorously moral an approach to life but he does bring with him his Christian categories of right and wrong and carries them with him off the boat along with his other belongings. Soon he feels the influence of the Sirocco. Soon he is influenced by the freer ways of the Nepentheans until at last he is forced to admit that he has reached a spiritual turning-point.

Something new had insinuated itself into his blood, some

demon of doubt and disquiet which threatened his old-established conceptions. Whence came it? The effect of changed environment – new friends, new food, new habits? The unaccustomed leisure which gave him, for the first time, a chance of thinking about non-professional matters? The South wind acting on his still weakened health? All these together? Or had he reached an epoch in his development, the termination of one of those definite life periods when all men worthy of the name pass through some cleansing process of spiritual desquamation, and slip their outworn weeds of thought and feeling?

In fact he is coming to learn what many Nepentheans have known for a long time, that most of the laws and beliefs of society are irrelevant and that all morality is relative. These themes are treated elsewhere in the book in situations not involving Heard, but his own 'conversion' is the most dramatic and the most lengthily considered. Soon he finds himself condoning the supposed immorality going on aboard Van Koppen's yacht and sharing Keith's humane attitude to the drunken Mrs Wilberforce. He listens with apparent approval to the Count's theories that climate may influence morals and that the Bible is a book which would naturally appeal to Goth or Anglo-Saxon but not to Nepenthean. But his final test comes when he sees his cousin Mrs Meadows murder her first husband, the obnoxious Muhlen, by pushing him over a cliff. Initially all his old values reassert themselves. ('Oh, it was villainous. How carefully the hour and place had been chosen.') Gradually, however, and with the aid of Keith, who believes that if Mrs Meadows ever committed a crime she would be right to do so, he begins to see the happening not simply as a murder but as a unique event. While the Nepenthean law is busy avoiding any action which will be harmful to its own smooth and corrupt running, Heard sees more and more the evil of the victim, the goodness of the murderer, the motivations behind her act. In the end he passes beyond forgiveness to admiration:

> Thinking thus, he not only understood. He approved. Mrs Meadows had saved her family. She was perfect of her kind.

If the climate and surroundings of Nepenthe have the effect of releasing men from the bondage of over-rigorous laws and morals, allowing them to value the unique and the beautiful above the laborious and the acceptable then (Count Caloveglia argues) any true Renaissance (and it will be a Renaissance for the few rather than the many) must take place in the Mediterranean area. There they would live among 'those whose business it is to bring the reasonableness of the few into its proper relief'. In the North, the very malevolence of the climate has encouraged men to glorify activity and the work ethic. As this is inevitable, the only course for the wise Northerner is to come south.

> That a man should wear himself to the bone in the acquisition of material gain is not pretty. But what else can he do in lands adapted only for wolves and bears? Without a degree of comfort which would be superfluous hereabouts he would feel humiliated. He must become strenuous if he wishes to rise superior to his inhospitable surroundings.

Freed from all this exhaustion of the body in the warmth of Nepenthe he can concentrate on the elevation of the mind.

Caloveglia puts the theory in its most extreme form, partly in order to evoke reactions from Heard, who is taking all this in with his usual sincere sobriety. But there is little doubt that Douglas did yearn for an exclusive meeting of superior minds such as this. He also strongly subscribed to the belief that surroundings and climate exert a profound and, largely unadmitted, influence on every one of us. That is why the influence of Nepenthe (Italy) is quite crucial in this book. Douglas's love of Southern Italy was in fact an obsession with him and so, when he makes Caloveglia say 'In the Mediterranean, Mr. Heard, lies the hope of humanity', we may be sure that the sentiment is not far from the author's own.

¶ Compton Mackenzie came to live for a period in Capri and Caterola. He met Douglas and without doubt *South Wind* influenced his two 'Mediterranean' books, *Vestal Fire* and *Extraordinary Women*. They are also set on an unidentified island, Sirene, which is near to Nepenthe and they share a number of themes and interests with Douglas's novel, not least the theory that the southern climate creates a more outgoing, less moralistic attitude among incomers. In *Extraordinary Women* Nature's power is conveyed very forcefully:

> We need not look beyond the sublime extravagances of the natural scene to account for the quickened pulses of Sirenians. When sun and moon enter into an alliance with earth and sky and sea to put mortals beside themselves, it is surely unnecessary to attribute the exciting quality of the air to rich deposits of radium.

In *Vestal Fire* the idea is related to that of 'expansion':

> And on that shady terrace you expanded. You expanded physically owing to the amount you had eaten and drunk . . . You expanded aesthetically as you gazed across a Bay of

Naples that was behaving as such famous views usually behave only in railway posters. You expanded historically as you tried to remember what exactly Nero did at Baiae . . . and you expanded morally, that is you became more elastic.

But in the exaggeration of the first passage and the wit of the second, you encounter the major difference between Douglas's approach and Mackenzie's. The latter prefers a lightly satiric mode. For him essentially the South is a place where sexual freedom is encouraged. *Vestal Fire* is dominated by homosexuals such as Nigel Dawson and above all the drug-taking Count Marsac. *Extraordinary Women* is dominated by lesbians – the self-centred Rosalba, the superior Olimpia Leigh and the pathetic Rory. Mackenzie at times enters their problems sympathetically but he is also ever ready to laugh at them and to point out (especially in the case of Marsac) how 'expansion' may lead to degradation. Around these vital, if bizarre, characters the home-based Sirenians can either adapt more naturally (Carlo) or cynically turn the visitors' desperate hedonistic adventures to their own monetary advantage (Alberto and Enrico Jones).

The two novels are themselves linked. Count Marsac, who has a major rôle in *Vestal Fire*, briefly enters *Extraordinary Women*, now entirely dependent on cocaine and a shadow of his former flamboyant self. Mme Sarbécoff, who has lived off her rings throughout *Vestal Fire*, sells her last one in *Extraordinary Women* and is forced to run a shop. Of the two, however, I think *Vestal Fire* proves the more successful, largely because the more serious focus on the elderly Pepworth-Nortons provides a more poignant ending than Rory's decision finally that she has outgrown her obsession with Rosalba and would instead like a cup of tea!

If, then, we look at *Vestal Fire* in relation to *South Wind*, we find the change of vision present on almost every level. Douglas had the erudite Eames working away harmlessly, obsessionally at his history of Nepenthe. But Sirene is full of absurd artists of one sort or another. Neave is translating Dante but dies without having finished *L'Inferno*; Scudamore aims at a work on Tiberius but first of all has to backtrack in order not to complete a work on Roman morals; Simon Pears writes a sonnet a day and so on. Eames was never as ludicrous as any of these. The bizarre origins of Saints' Legends were explored in *South Wind* but there was nothing as outrageously hilarious as the battle between San Mercurio and San Bonzo in Chapter 5 of *Vestal Fire*. Literary and historical knowledge, seriously treated by Douglas as part of the Italian cultural heritage, sometimes becomes in Mackenzie's books a mere excuse for intellectual one-upmanship. Thus, when the men are all dining on flamingoes at Marsac's 'pink' banquet Dr Mewburn compares it to Trimalchio's feast; Scudamore replies by quoting Martial; Neave inevitably tries to top this with Dante and Marsac introduces Plato's *Symposium* before the whole fatuous exercise is undercut by Pears who wishes to praise his epic on Red Indians.

But amidst all this light satire, there is the touching story of the two elderly cousins Miss Virginia and Miss Maimie Pepworth-Norton. Sometimes they too are objects of our mirth and Miss Virginia's insecure grasp of Italian at moments of stress is particularly amusing:

> Rosina, mettere questa signorina – oh hell, Maimie, I wish I knew the Italian for a mean ordinary little sneak – mettere questa signorina chi è niente signorina fuori. Subito! Subito! Subito!

But their sincerely held paganism contrasts with the exotic 'pagan' exploits of such as Marsac. Their meeting with him at the temple of Vesta and unflinching loyalty to his cause until at last his viciousness is made so clear that even they are forced to see it, is in its own way heroic. Above all, while many of the others understand Sirene (Italy) only superficially and deserve the contempt with which they are secretly treated, the Pepworth-Nortons' understanding of and love for the country is almost as great as the undying love they have for each other. It is therefore in every way fitting that beneath the romanesque window in the cemetery wall, there is the simple inscription:

> Within this bit of foreign earth
> there lies
> The dust of Two
> Who loved this Italy.

Italy itself plays almost as important a part in Mackenzie's novels as in *South Wind*, seriousness blending with frivolity to give a more varied if less profound picture.

¶ Of our modern novelists the one who has the closest connections with Italy is Muriel Spark, who has now settled there. Many of her novels use Italian material but an analysis of three – *The Prime of Miss Jean Brodie* (1961); *The Public Image* (1968) and *The Takeover* (1976) – will go some way to establishing the artistry with which she uses her knowledge of the land, its history and culture. The latter two are set in Italy, while Miss Brodie's fertile imagination, when not confined to the realities of Edinburgh takes many a flight south to that land where she habitually spent her summer holidays.

Although the precise nature of the Italian contribution differs in these three works, there is no doubt that for Mrs Spark the precise setting of her novels usually reinforces their dominant theme. She has herself stated that her conversion to Catholicism freed her artistic impulses and this in its turn has resulted in writing which is ultimately allegorical in the sense that it is a fictional representation of a perceived truth. Everything, there-fore, fits into a planned pattern, although the organisation may be as tight and spare as in *The Public Image* or as loosely episodic as in *The Takeover.*

Chronologically *The Prime of Miss Jean Brodie* is the first of the three. Its setting is Edinburgh and this is fitting because of that city's connections with John Knox and Calvinism. Just as Calvin-ism is a religion of the few chosen and the many damned, so Miss Brodie chooses and grooms her select group of children in Marcia Blaine School for Girls. Set as she is in a city which in many ways reflects her own basic creed, her imagination nonetheless regularly finds respite in Italy. There is first of all the Italy of the past; the most powerful element in that general cultural education in which she specialises and which sets her apart from the other, more conventional teachers. Inevitably her own tastes dominate, so that although the Brodie girls alone learn of the great Italian Renaissance painters, judgments of relative value are Miss Brodie's alone:

'Who is the greatest Italian painter?'

'Leonardo da Vinci, Miss Brodie.'

'That is incorrect. The answer is Giotto, he is my favourite.'
As increasingly the anecdotes concerning her own life become flavoured with the fantasies born of frustration, so they can effortlessly become intertwined with culture, and a culture which is usually Italian:

I shall tell you a little more about Italy. I met a young poet by a fountain. Here is a picture of Dante meeting Beatrice.

But just as she draws from the Italian past, so her worship of the strong and the talented turns naturally to fascism and the Italian present:

Sandy recalled Miss Brodie's admiration for Mussolini's marching troops, and the picture she had brought back from Italy showing the triumphant march of the black uniforms in Rome.

Then finally she is dismissed. The official reason is that she has been teaching fascism and there is the necessary grain of truth in this, which makes the charge stick. On one level Miss Brodie is Marcia Blaine's Mussolini, with her chosen 'fascisti' but she is much more than this. A creature of light and shade, living on the borderline between reality and illusion, she is fittingly set not only against the contrasting backgrounds of Edinburgh and Italy but also against Italy's own contrasts – flourishing romantic past and narrow, dictator-ridden present. Thus she is in a sense both defined by these backgrounds and excused by them, becoming in the end much more a human object of sympathy than the personification of a vilified creed.

The Public Image is predominantly set in Rome and tells of the rise to fame of a moderately talented actress, Annabel Christopher. She has correctly been called an atypical Spark heroine because she is neither intelligent nor sensitive nor witty. But she is *determined*, sacrificing all to her career and the false images of her projected by the publicity men. In the end, after her husband's suicide, she re-finds herself, ironically through loving that baby which had initially been conceived to reinforce the image.

This is a work in which every extraneous detail has been excised, and this principle extends to the setting. Rome is not described to us. Its value lies in the outlook of its inhabitants and particularly two obsessively highlighted traits. One of these permits Annabel to gain her fame and the other encourages her to maintain it at the expense of lost identity. The first is the Italian's ability to see things in clearcut black and white. This, the narrator informs us, stems from the old Mediaeval categories of self examination. Once accepted, it permits images of vice and virtue not only to be presented in the magazines but to hold the popular imagination:

> Sheer villains, utter innocents – the world's most complicated celebrities have been cast anew in these simple roles. In fact it is only a country of dramatic history, cradled in the Seven Capital Sins, that could so full-heartedly produce this popular art-form.

The second is the Italian love of acting; the readiness to accept the appearance for the reality. Annabel is manufactured by the Italian film industry. She is true not to herself but to what she must seem to be. Inevitably she finds succour from a people who place so much faith in appearance:

> The neighbours were silent, upholding that principle of appearance appropriate to an occasion which they called *bella figura*

and prefer what should be to what is:

> And the more sophisticated readers simply repeated the Italian proverb 'If it isn't true, it's to the point'.

Thus, as in *The Prime of Miss Jean Brodie,* the setting is not incidental to the major character, it is in a sense an extension of her. It is no arbitrary twist of plot, that once Annabel has at last found sincerity, she catches a plane for Greece. Italy and Italian values have become the emblem of her old self, its posturing, its whiter than white image. The pilgrimage is at once spiritual and geographic. She not only leaves her old self; she also leaves behind the country which nurtured it and shared its values.

Although there is not nearly so clearcut a link between setting and theme in *The Takeover,* the two are again interrelated. The lush surroundings of Nemi are described more than once and their influence on Sir James Frazer's study of Comparative Religion, established:

> incredible fertility . . . A little to the North was a corner of Hubert's roof, and under the cliff below him at a point where the banks of the lake spread less steeply into a small plain lay the cultivated furrowed and planted small fields of flowers and the dark green density of woodland that covers what Fraser in *The Golden Bough* described as the scene of the tragedy.

The last reference leads us on to the various legends centring on the Tauric Diana, especially the one that she was abducted by the mad Emperor Caligula and that offspring of this match between Goddess and mortal still exist.

This legend is worked into the central story-line. Maggie Radcliffe from the beginning to the end of the novel is trying to evict from one of her villas her erstwhile friend Hubert Mallindaine. Hubert, as his name ('maligne Diane') suggests, chooses to believe more ancient grounds for possession – that he is himself one of Diana's offspring:

> 'Nemi,' said Hubert, leaning back in the chair with his legs stretched out wide in front of him. 'Nemi is mine. It belongs to me, as a matter of fact. The offspring of Diana and Caligula became the high priest of Diana's sanctuary and I am his descendant.'

Less obviously, the vision of nature presented by Nemi, *The Golden Bough* and the legend of Diana is in complete harmony with the attitudes of the characters and the moral of the tale told by Mrs Spark.

The relationship is subtle and the associations many. Space permits me only to name two. The Diana of Nemi has become a goddess of fertility. In Nemi, that excessively fertile land, love is open, free and pursued in an essentially pagan spirit. The most explicit statement on this comes from Hubert ('Copulation has always been part of the worship and propitiation of nature. . . . Your Christianity is simply a passing phase.'), but even a character so apparently conventional as the determinedly Anglo-Saxon Mary finds Lauro's attempted rape so enjoyable that she 'yielded after the first gasp'.

But the other vision of Diana the dominant huntress is also maintained. Nemi is not only fertile it is also natural, and being natural reflects a life of conflict with victory going to those most capable of adaptation. Throughout, this Bergsonian vision is supported by the details of the story but most obviously at the conclusion, when Hubert and Maggie the arch-rivals meet in friendly fashion to share versions of their different victories. Hubert has come through because, although evicted, he has sold all Maggie's expensive furniture and paintings, replacing them with fakes. Maggie has gained her revenge on the man who ruined her, by having him kidnapped and recouping the money lost through ransom. It is a particularly sophisticated version of 'nature red in tooth and claw' but that it is nonetheless.

The Nemi of fertility and adaptation, the Rome of posturing and allegoric vision, the cultural and Fascistic Italies of Miss Brodie's experience and imagination – all these in their different ways are part of what Mrs Spark calls 'the imaginative extensions of truth', emerging from her novels. They are necessary parts of the patterns in an art which manages at once to be witty and profound.

¶ Eric Linklater's *Private Angelo*, begun in Rome in August 1944 and completed in Orkney exactly a year later, deals with the Second World War and the liberation of Italy. The daring (and successful) step he takes is to view the events predominantly through the puzzled eyes of an Italian soldier. The tone is predominantly comic but for all his lightness of approach Linklater gradually shows us that Private Angelo, whom we are tempted at first to dismiss as a coward, has greater strength and a deeper vision than most of the more active, militant forces around him. That courage and depth of vision is inextricably linked with the country which bore him, as puzzled as he is but just as vital.

The essential problem is one of re-definition. At the beginning we as readers, as well as Angelo himself, think he lacks courage. That indeed is the topic of the book's opening sentence:

> 'The trouble with you, Angelo,' said the Count severely, 'is that you lack the "dono di coraggio".'

But as the story progresses we learn that although he has not much stomach for military endeavour or physical confrontations, he has a different courage, the courage of endurance, of 'pazi-enza'. The Allies too come to understand this and in the very last chapter Major Telfer confides to a friend that even though Italians like Angelo may sometimes run from the battle line, they are capable of coming through the worst privations with their will to live as strong as ever. 'It's their own sort of courage,' he concludes, 'but they've got it.'

Linklater, then, tries not only to contrast the Italian outlook with the English, the American and the German, but through Angelo he begins to persuade us that it is in many vital ways superior. The first superiority is that of resilience and adaptation, a capacity which arises in the first instance from the refusal to see things as neatly as the English or the Germans do. The latter frequently come to the same simple, condescending conclusions about the Italians but from completely opposed premises. The friendly young German officer thinks they feel guilty because they have broken the alliance. Major Telfer thinks they feel guilty and ashamed because they were decisively beaten. But Angelo and his fellow Italians do not give the impression of guilt but of sane bewilderment wondering how best to accommodate itself to a mad world. In military terms it may seem that Angelo who fights at one time or another for three different armies is at best a coward, at worst a traitor. In fact he is reacting to forces beyond his control, while all the time cherishing the deeper values of love and a reverence for life. In moral terms, it means that his affection for Lucrezia continues to flourish despite in-fidelity and rape, the sort of circumstances which would have destroyed it for more conventional men. In a way all this is summed up in a brief conversation between Don Agesilas and the Countess at a time when the Liberation is clearly succeeding. 'What's happened to all the Fascists?' he asks. And she replies 'Many of them have become Communists.'

But this resilience only becomes admirable because it is linked to a vision which is both higher and more mature than that of the competing armies. For Linklater, Italy is still the land of ancient beauty and ancient culture. It is, therefore, symbolic, that Angelo for all his changes of side continually protects Piero della Fran-cesca's 'Adoration of the Shepherds'. At the end, although it has been mutilated he retains the head and hangs it triumphantly on the kitchen wall. To this appreciation of cultural values is added an awareness of spiritual ones. At the height of liberation, when Americans and British receive their 'plaudits' like 'actors', the Count points out whom the Romans are really thanking:

    . . . not for a moment do they believe that either the Americans or the English wrote the play. No, indeed! And that is why they have been saving their enthusiasm, and why they are going to show it now. For now they are going to shout for the author.

To the Pope and God go Italy's true thanks. If this represents the greater height of the Italian vision, its greater maturity is reflected mainly in their satirical, clear-eyed vision of what the allies see as liberation carefully planned but Angelo and his friends as destruction fortuitously scattered. The allies attack Cassino and nearly kill Angelo, who is miles away:

'Do I in any way, resemble Cassino?' he asked Simon, as soon as he was allowed to visit him.

'There is no apparent similarity,' Simon answered.

'Then why was I bombed?'

'We all make mistakes from time to time.'

'We do not all carry bombs. To make a private mistake in your own house is one thing, but to make a public mistake with a bomb of two hundred and fifty kilogrammes is different altogether.'

And finally, partly because of these powers of resilience and clear vision, but also because of their very will to live and love, Linklater argues, in terms so very different from Douglas's Count Caloveglia, that in the Italian outlook and setting lies the hope for the future. Circumstances give Angelo four children to look after. One is his, one an Englishman's, one a Pole's and another a Moor's. He accepts the facts that have led up to this and hopes that the arrangement may help to break down chauvinism and 'demonstrate that all the people of the world – or four of them at least – can make their home together in civilisation.' As he points out this family and the fertility of the Italian countryside to Major Telfer at the end, we see peace emerging from war, love from hatred. And for the first time we appreciate fully the force of the Count's earlier claim:

Nations totter, empires crumble . . . but man is invincible, man is the true phoenix, and our dear Italy is the home of the *risorgimento*, the renaissance, the indefeasible and recurrent spring of beauty.

And of all that – unpromising, unassuming Angelo is the worthy embodiment.

¶ The last novel I wish to consider is by Allan Massie, one of the best authors writing in Scotland today. *The Death of Men* is set in Italy and avowedly based on the recent abduction and murder of Aldo Moro. We do not, however, directly hear the views of Dusa

(Moro), but listen instead to the reactions of three carefully chosen onlookers. These at first seem to fill foreseeable and contrasted positions. Dusa's brother, Raimundo, is drawn to the leader through ties of family and anxious to gain his release. Tomaso the idealistic revolutionary in part masterminds the abduction and so wishes his destruction. The neutral journalist Christopher is interested only in obtaining a good story. But by the end we learn that, albeit in different ways, all three have come to admire Dusa and been surprised by the mature way in which he handled the impossible situation in which he found himself. Interestingly too, while Raimundo becomes less emotionally involved as time goes by, seeing the futility of any positive action; Tomaso, in conversation with Dusa, is so infected by his views and his personality that he finally loses faith in everything and kills himself.

Thus the form of the novel lends itself to a subtle presentation of a drama working at once on personal and political levels. Nor would it be accurate to say that in all senses it is a drama which could only be fought out on Italian soil. The self-interested plottings of Dusa's supposed supporters in parliament; the naive idealism of the revolutionaries and the various contradictory theories of what constitutes political progress may be decked out in Italian costume but essentially they are problems and postures of universal relevance.

On the other hand, many of those elements which are recognisably Italian prove to be those we have met already in the works of Douglas, Mackenzie, Spark and Linklater although the context and the mode of handling is different. For example, although Massie does not obviously subscribe to Douglas's theory of a 'climatic morality', he does present Italy as a place where homosexuality, lesbianism and pederasty are common:

> A figure appeared at the window, a younger figure than the American's and slimmer, with an aureole of curls framing an oval face. I sensed rather than truly saw his nakedness. The American approached from behind, laid an arm around the shoulder and drew the boy away from the window, drew him downwards and out of sight.

This is not a very important line in the novel but it does continue a preoccupation shared by Douglas and Mackenzie.

Like Muriel Spark, on whose work he has written authoritatively, Massie seizes on the vast difference between reality and appearance in Italian society. Again, while this was a governing theme behind *Private Image*, it is only once mentioned explicitly in *The Death of Men*. But that explicit comment comes at the very end of the novel when Raimundo is summing up Italy's 'actor-like' reaction to his brother's death and it has been implicit in many previous passages:

> Ten days since it happened. Since they did it. And today, in a grand orgy of hypocrisy, Italy remembers the man they did nothing to save.

Characteristically, although this seems to be a grand conclusion, the facts are not so simple. Some characters, like Tomaso, have found their own way to sincerity, while Raimundo's readiness to include himself in the universal condemnation paradoxically calls into question the universal validity of his own judgment.

This is Massie's way. He invites generalisations only to frustrate them with a keenness of insight, which arguably was even better displayed in *The Last Peacock*. Thus, in comparing Italian ways with English, he and Linklater may sometimes agree (e.g. on the Italian's greater spiritual awareness), sometimes disagree (e.g. on the seriousness with which Italians and English view politics), but Massie is never sweeping in his judgments. Thus Elena and others are thrilled that the Pope is going to appeal on Dusa's behalf, but Raimundo believes that 'We all seek earthly crowns'. Bella (incidentally contradicting Linklater's Countess) may lament 'One thing I liked about England though was that there was no politics. You couldn't imagine anyone killing for politics', but the very fact that she laments the situation shows her position to be apart from the norm. *Private Angelo* had consistently upheld the particular value that Italians put on the family and their ability to accept with resignation situations which would destroy the best men of other nations. Throughout his long torment Dusa finds his strength in the family:

> Instead he was turning back to that eternal Italian reality, the only thing we are prepared to trust, the Family.

and when he dies Tomaso comments:

> So, with Southern resignation . . . he surrendered to the effective, the dominant Will.

Yet the same Dusa is destroyed by a member of that family; one who places the state above blood relationships. And the very Tomaso who pronounces that benediction proceeds to take the most 'unresigned' action of all, in killing himself.

Massie does not deny the generalisations that the earlier authors had set up when contemplating Italian life, but he reveals them *as* generalisations, often making the exceptions an ironic comment on their inherent oversimplification. The world he presents is a more troubled and complex one, certainly than that of Douglas or Mackenzie. But in providing this new and stimulating voice, he strengthens that varied group of novelists, who have made sure that the richness of Italian influence on twentieth-century Scottish Literature should not be confined to poetry.

Bibliography of Scottish Authors

The Field

Gavin Douglas: *The Shorter Poems of Gavin Douglas*, ed. Priscilla Bawcutt, Scottish Text Society, 1967.

Robert Henryson: *The Poems of Robert Henryson*, ed. Denton Fox (Oxford, 1981).

David Lindsay: *The Works of Sir David Lindsay of the Mount*, ed. Douglas Hamer, Scottish Text Society, 4 vols., 1931-6.

?John Reid: *The Thre Prestis of Peblis*, ed. T. D. Robb, Scottish Text Society, 1915.

James VI and the First Renaissance

William Alexander: *The Poetical Works of Sir William Alexander*, ed. L. E. Kastner, H. B. Charlton, Scottish Text Society, 1929.

Robert Ayton: *The Works of Sir Robert Ayton*, ed. Charles Gullans, Scottish Text Society, 1963.

Alexander Craig: *The Poetical Works of Alexander Craig of Rosecraig*, ed. David Laing, Hunterian Club, 1873.

William Drummond: *William Drummond of Hawthornden: Poems and Prose*, ed. Robert H. MacDonald (Edinburgh and London, 1976).

William Fowler: *The Works of William Fowler*, ed. Henry Meikle et al., Scottish Text Society, 3 vols., 1914-40.

James VI and I: *The Poems of King James VI of Scotland*, ed. J. Craigie, Scottish Text Society, 2 vols., 1948-52.

David Murray: *The Poems of Sir David Murray of Gorthy*, ed. T. Kinnear, Abbotsford Club, 1823.

John Stewart: *The Poems of John Stewart of Baldynneis*, ed. T. Crockett, Scottish Text Society, 1913.

The Eighteenth and Nineteenth Centuries

James Boswell: *Boswell on the Grand Tour: Italy, Corsica and France (1765-66)*, ed. F. Brady and F. Pottle (London, 1955).

Robert Burns: *The Poems and Songs of Robert Burns*, ed. James Kinsley, 3 vols. (Oxford, 1968). (Also in Paperback, single volume edition.)

Lord Byron: *Complete Poetical Works*, ed. J. J. McGann, 3 vols. (Oxford, 1981).

Robert Fergusson: *The Poems of Robert Fergusson*, ed. M. P. McDiarmid, Scottish Text Society, 2 vols., 1954-6.

William Hamilton: *The Poems and Songs of W.H.*, ed. James Paterson (Edinburgh, 1850).

David Hume: *The Letters of David Hume*, ed. J. Y. T. Greig, 2 vols. (Oxford, 1932).

Alexander Pennecuick: *A Collection of Scots Poems on several occasions* (Glasgow, 1787).

Allan Ramsay: *The Works of Allan Ramsay*, ed. Burns Martin et al., Scottish Text Society, 3 vols., 1944-55.

Walter Scott: There are many convenient paperback editions of Scott's major novels in the Penguin, Collins Classics and Everyman series, for example. My quotations follow the Oxford 24 volume edition of the *Works* (Oxford, 1912).

Adam Smith: *Essays on Philosophical Subjects* (Basle, 1799).

—— *Lectures on Rhetoric and Belles Lettres*, ed. J. M. Lothian (London, 1963).

Tobias Smollett: *The Adventures of Ferdinand Count Fathom*, ed. Damian Grant (London, 1971).

—— *The Adventures of Peregrine Pickle*, ed. J. L. Clifford (London, 1964).

—— *The Adventures of Roderick Random*, ed. P.-G. Boucé (Oxford, 1979).

—— *The Expedition of Humphry Clinker*, ed. L. M. Knapp (London, 1966).

—— *The Life and Adventures of Sir Lancelot Greaves*, ed. David Evans (London, 1973).

—— *Travels through France and Italy*, ed. F. Felsenstein (Oxford, 1979).

James Thomson (1700-48): *The Complete Poetical Works*, ed. J. Logie Robertson (Oxford, 1908).

James Thomson ('B.V.') (1834-82): *The Poems of James Thomson*, ed. G. H. Gerould (New York, 1927).

Thomas Urquhart: *The Jewel*, ed. R. D. S. Jack and R. J. Lyall (Edinburgh, 1983).

The Second Renaissance

Victor Carin: *The Servant o' Twa Maisters* (Royal Lyceum Acting Copy).

Norman Douglas: *Old Calabria* (London, 1915), (modern edition, Century).

—— *Siren Land* (London, 1911), (modern edition, Secker and Warburg).

—— *South Wind* (London, 1917), (modern edition, Secker and Warburg).

Robin Fulton: *An Italian Quartet* (London, 1966).

Robert Garioch: *Complete Poetical Works*, ed. Robin Fulton (Edinburgh, 1983).

Hamish Henderson: *Elegies for the dead in Cyrenaica* (Edinburgh, 1977).

—— *Gramsci*, 2 vols. (Edinburgh, 1974).

—— Ruggero Orlando, 'On Contemporary Italian Poetry', *New Road*, 1946.

Eric Linklater: *Private Angelo* (London, 1946).

—— *The Campaign in Italy* (London, 1951).

Compton Mackenzie: *Extraordinary Women* (London, 1928).

—— *Vestal Fire* (London, 1927).

Allan Massie: *The Death of Men* (London, 1981).

Edwin Morgan: *Fifty Renascence Love Poems* (Reading, 1975).

—— (In) *Lyric Poetry of the Italian Renaissance*, ed. R. L. Lind (New Haven, 1964).

—— *Poems from Eugenio Montale* (Reading, 1959).

—— *Rites of Passage* (Manchester, 1976).

Muriel Spark: *The Prime of Miss Jean Brodie* (London, 1961).

—— *The Public Image* (London, 1970).

—— *The Takeover* (London, 1976). See also *Loitering with Intent* (1981) and *Territorial Rights* (1961).

Index of References to
Italian Authors